THE
NEXT LEVEL

Leading Beyond the Status Quo

DAVID COTTRELL
WITH ALICE ADAMS

THE NEXT LEVEL
LEADING BEYOND THE STATUS QUO

Printed in the United States of America
ISBN: 0-9772257-3-9

Credits
Design, art direction, and production   Melissa Monogue, Back Porch Creative, Plano, TX
info@BackPorchCreative.com

CONTENTS

INTRODUCTION

"What does it take to get to the Next Level?"

You hear this question in almost every board room and meeting room, regardless of industry or current performance: How can we move our organization to the Next Level?

Actually, there's nothing magical about getting to the Next Level. Every person and organization eventually reaches a Next Level. It may not be the Next Level you envision because we all expect the Next Level to be higher and greater … but it could be lower and lesser – a Next Level that may even lead to going out of business or out of a job.

The real question is: **What steps can we take so the Next Level is higher and greater … accomplishing both personal and organizational goals?**

This book shows you how to move beyond the status quo and out of the comfort of complacency to achieve your objectives. This story of a 5K race, will help you discover that in running, as well as running your organization, moving upward to the Next Level requires dedication, discipline, hard work and a systematic process.

The Next Level begins with you! When you create an atmosphere where your team believes the reward of moving upward to the Next Level is worth the effort ... then you will achieve results beyond any you can envision.

Enjoy the story, share the lessons with everyone in your organization, attack the status quo and move forward to a higher and greater Next Level!

REQUIREMENTS TO REACH THE NEXT LEVEL

"There is at least one point in the history of any company when you have to change dramatically to rise to the Next Level of performance. Miss that moment – and you start to decline."
– Andrew S. Grove, former Chairman, Intel Corp.

"I see our first finisher rounding the corner, ladies and gentleman ... and yes, we have a repeat winner this year. Here he comes now ... Michael Burney clocking a personal best of six minutes, 15 seconds a mile today," the loudspeaker blared.

Fans on both sides of the race course cheered as Burney, the vice president of finance for a large corporation, was first to cross the finish line after completing a grueling 5K course, assuring victory for his team. Behind him came his competitors, many of them much younger than Burney's 50 years.

The city's annual corporate challenge traditionally attracted several dozen teams to compete in a variety of competitions ... swimming, cycling, tennis and track. Today's 5K marked the culmination of the events and would determine the final winner.

As the remainder of the 200 runners finished the race, a number of the younger runners crowded around Burney at the refreshment pavilion, congratulating him as they gulped down Gatorade to rehydrate themselves.

Don Martin and Randy Moore were on Burney's winning team but sat dejectedly, reviewing their race times as they ate bananas and bagels. "Man, this isn't good. I started this race way too fast and by the second mile was sucking wind," Randy said, shaking his head. "According to my stopwatch, I was only pumping out about one mile every eight minutes. That's pathetic."

"Don't feel bad," said Don, stuffing the last of a bagel into his mouth. "I finished behind you."

"But, I really worked to do better than that. I trained … hard … for months," Randy whined.

"Months? Man, I thought you had to travel most of the last two months?"

"Well, yes … but I ran every Saturday morning … and I did weight training whenever I could."

"Hey guys … hurting already?" Michael Burney, who was once their boss before he took over the financial division, had spied them in the corner and was coming their way. "Man, it was a great day for a race. Not too hot, not too humid," he said.

"Not as far as I'm concerned," Don drawled. "But, hey. We need to thank you for pulling our team to victory. Too bad we weren't more help. Without your time, we'd be dead last."

Burney could see the disappointment on the young men's faces. "It's all about the team," he said. "I just wanted to do my part."

"That's the problem," Don responded. "Neither of us feel we contributed very much. Let's face it; our times were some of the worst. We were just sitting here admiring you … we don't know how you do it. Every year your time gets a little better – just enough to stay ahead of the rest of the pack."

Michael took the towel he had around his neck and wiped his forehead. "Thanks for the kind words. Mind if I sit down?"

"Oh … no … sure … have a seat."

"This corporate challenge is all about having fun and competing against some of our business competitors," Michael explained. "Of course, what we do on the race course has little to do with how we do business, but there are some real lessons I have learned from this competition. Lessons that have helped me make better decisions at work."

Both of the younger men looked puzzled.

"Does it really bother you that your times fell short of your expectations?" Michael asked.

"Well … I," Randy fumbled for the right words. "I thought I was prepared to run much better than I did … so I'm more than a little disappointed," he admitted.

"Same here," Don echoed. "I want to improve, but it's just not happening for me."

"Tell you what," Michael continued. "If you are serious about improving, I'd be willing to train with you. About five years ago, I found myself sitting in this same corner after that year's challenge – I think it was the first 5K I had entered. My time was so dismal and I was so humiliated, I didn't stay around for the awards presentation. I was humiliated because not only had I let the team down but I let myself down."

The two men sitting across from him leaned forward. They could relate to what he was saying.

"So, I made it my goal to improve my time before the next challenge and I went to work," Michael said. "I worked with a coach who helped me make some changes in my lifestyle. I also worked really hard on my own. I suffered some real pain, but I also made some significant gains … and the next year, I not only took my race time to the Next Level, I won the 5K."

"A coach?" Don wondered. "You worked with a coach?"

"Most people learn through experience, but having a coach helps too," Michael said. "If you look at professional sports, you'll see that the world's greatest athletes have coaches. Everyone needs a coach, but nothing replaces your personal desire or effort.

"Let me tell you a story about coaching – and no fair rolling your eyes. I don't know if you're into classical music or not, but I happen to love the music of Pablo Casals, one of the great cellists of the last century.

"When Pablo Casals reached 95, a young reporter asked him, 'Mr. Casals, you are 95 and still you practice six hours a day and work with a teacher. Why do you, perhaps the greatest cellist that ever lived, still practice and work with a master teacher … a coach?'

"And, Mr. Casals answered, 'Because I think I'm making progress.'

"The moral of my story – if you want to reach the Next Level in your running – or anything else – your goal is to make FORWARD progress every day.

"Anyway, if you're interested in raising the bar on your performance, I am willing to help. We can meet the first Saturday morning of every month at the high school track and train together," he said. "There's nothing lonelier than running five miles by yourself, so I'd love some company … and we can learn from each other. I may have some of the answers, but not all of them, and – like you – I'm always looking to take my game to the Next Level."

"Great," Don said. "I'll be there."

"Me too," Randy said, finishing his second banana. "As you can tell from my time, I definitely need some help."

"Want to start next Saturday morning … say 7 a.m. sharp?" Michael asked. "I'll tell you now … it's gonna take work … and I'm going to ask you to make a deal with me."

"A deal?" asked Randy, grinning nervously.

"You're going to find that there are a tremendous number of parallels between improving your running ability and increasing your business performance. Because of those parallels, I'm going to ask you to apply what you learn on the track to your life at work or at home and share the results each time we meet. Running is great, but learning and applying what you discover from our time together is what's important."

"I can do that," Randy agreed, "and that may be the easiest part."

"Sounds good," Don said, shaking hands with Michael and Randy and then picking up his gym bag. "I am looking forward to learning from the best."

REQUIREMENTS TO REACH THE NEXT LEVEL

1. Desire to improve

2. Understand there is room for improvement

3. Confidence that positive change can happen

STEPPING UP TO
THE CHALLENGE

*"If you want to take your mission in life to the Next Level,
look inside. Abolish your fears and raise your commitment
level to the point of no return, and I guarantee you that
the champion within will propel you toward victory."*
– Olympian Bruce Jenner

At 7 a.m. the next Saturday, Michael Burney was at the high school track. Don Martin came jogging across the field a few minutes after 7 a.m and Randy Moore was right behind him.

"Before we start our session," Michael began, "I'd like to make a point. If you're serious about improving your running and committed to paying the price for improvement, you need to be here on time. That's 7 a.m sharp. That said, now I'd like to hear what each of you expects out of our training sessions."

Randy was the first to speak: "Plain and simple. I'd like to turn in a decent time at the next corporate challenge 5K. This year was embarrassing."

Don nodded and said, "I'm in the same boat. I'd like to reach the Next Level in my running."

"Okay. Both are good goals," Michael agreed, "but I'd like for you to be more specific. Don, what exactly does the Next Level mean for you? Where is it? Does that mean you want to get a few seconds better or a few minutes better?"

"Hmmm. Good question," Don said after a few thoughtful moments. "I'd definitely like to improve my time more than a few seconds. This last race I ran close to a nine-minute mile pace. There was a guy about twice my age who ran faster. I'd like to trim my time back to a seven-minute mile … or less … if that's possible."

"That's a good beginning," Michael agreed. "So, for you the Next Level is about seven minutes per mile?"

Don nodded.

"But, is that really the Next Level for you?"

"I'm not sure I know what you're getting at."

Michael smiled. "It's tough to work with abstractions, but let's see if we can make your goals even more specific. With enough training, I have no doubt you'll eventually shave a couple of minutes off every mile, but when you finish the race, how do you want to feel? You can be totally exhausted and take a couple of days to recover or you can feel exhilarated by the workout.

"Moving to the Next Level means improving performance … and not just part of the performance. When you reach the Next Level, you've improved a series of events – like how efficiently you prepare, how you feel while you're running the race, how fast you run the race and how long it takes you to recover.

"The Next Level isn't one step. It's a series of steps."

His protégés were thoughtful. "The Next Level – in anything – is more than one element of your performance. It's the big picture," Randy repeated.

"It's the same in business as it is in running," Michael explained. "Remember when we wanted to take our marketing program to the Next Level?" His question was rhetorical. "We didn't just hire new salespeople and broaden our territories. We evaluated the situation and then increased our product line, took a more efficient approach to selling, trained our customer service staff and spent more time qualifying our customers. The new marketing program took us to the Next Level because we changed our big picture."

The two men nodded.

"Moving to the Next Level involves the same steps," pointed out their mentor:

- ✦ Set your goal
- ✦ Evaluate the situation
- ✦ Equip yourself
- ✦ Endure while improving
- ✦ Reevaluate performance
- ✦ Evacuate comfort zones
- ✦ Stick to your strategy
- ✦ Set your new goal

"That makes a lot of sense," Randy nodded. "In fact, we've started work on the first step this morning – setting our goals."

"Absolutely," Michael agreed. "But, a word of caution here. When we decide to move to the Next Level, we don't always move up."

"You mean it's a double-edged sword?" Don spoke up.

"I'll have to give you a 'yes and no' answer on that one," Michael apologized. "In order to reach a goal, sometimes you need to move down a notch in order to perfect a style or to gain a skill you might be missing. Taking a step back is often necessary for you to eventually move up.

"Let me give you an example. Ever heard of Ping golf clubs?"

The guys nodded. "Best putter I've ever had," Don said.

"At age 50, Karsten Solheim took up the game of golf, and like many of us, he began looking for ways to take his game to the Next Level.

"Solheim was a mechanical engineer with General Electric, so he began looking at the mechanics of the game – particularly his putter's construction. He set up a shop in his garage and started working to design what he believed to be a superior putter by putting most of the weight in the toe and heel of the putter and leaving the middle almost a shell. He made his first putter in 1958.

"Because it made a 'ping' sound when his putter met the ball, he called his new invention 'the Ping Putter.'

"One of Solheim's favorite sayings was, 'Why don't you try it?' He was always encouraging other golfers to try out his putters. That kept him busy in his garage shop, making his putters by hand.

"Almost every golfer who saw the Ping Putter wanted one, and soon requests were coming in from pro shops across the nation – all without any advertising or marketing.

"In 1967, Karsten Solheim decided to take a step back. He left a lucrative career at General Electric to devote his full attention to building putters, eventually moving from his garage to a small manufacturing shop. All the while, he was evaluating processes, inventing new ones and creating new products. Each new process and every new product required taking a step back before moving ahead.

"Solheim once admitted his parents told him he was out of his mind to leave GE after investing 15 years with the company." Then, he added, "But, it turned out pretty well. A year after his death, Karsten was named to the PGA's Golfing Hall of Fame."

"That's a great story," Don said, "and I see your point. Reaching the Next Level sometimes means taking a step back before moving forward."

"Right," Michael said. "And, Karsten Solheim chose a higher level than other manufacturers. In whatever we do, whether it's running or how we're doing our jobs … we choose our own Next Level.

"Now, before the sun gets much higher, let's do three things," Michael suggested. "First, I'll show you what I do to stretch and warm-up. Then, let's go on an easy run – about eight laps around the track. After that, I'll show you a good way to cool down and then we can talk about what we'll do before our next workout."

"Warm up, run and cool down. I normally just take off and run. You have already changed my process for training," Randy said. "Let's get going."

———————————

After a 15-minute warm-up, the trio began their laps around the track … their initial pace was a slow but steady jog.

"You know, you're on the right pace if you can carry on a conversation as you run without getting winded," said Michael, taking his place between the two younger runners. "Let's try it because I also wanted to talk to you about something called 'the first date fallacy.'

"Here's how it goes … you meet someone, decide to go on a first date and everything goes just fine. At the end of the evening, your date assures you it was wonderful and wants to see you again – soon. You feel the same way.

"Then you wonder, 'What if I seem too eager. Maybe I should wait a few days to call.' Then you might think, 'If she really wanted to see me, wouldn't she call?' Three days pass. Then five. Naturally, you assume that, despite what your instincts (and what your date told you the first time out), there's no interest. Meanwhile, your date has assumed the same of you, figuring that if you were interested, you would have called.

"What's missing in this fledgling relationship is the same thing absent from a lot of our efforts to reach the Next Level – a clear direction of what the next step is. It's great to have goals and aspirations, but often we find ourselves paralyzed – stuck at the same level of performance."

Michael noticed that both Don and Randy weren't saying much. "You guys doing okay?"

They nodded in unison although it was clear Don was beginning to breath heavily and with his mouth open. Michael slowed the pace.

"In the past, we've had leaders in our company who could really inspire our employees to work hard, reach higher and really want to move to the Next Level. Then, once they were hooked, their leaders neglected to reel them in by giving them the right focus, tools, feedback and the right encouragement to move forward. The employees had inspiration but they were also looking for direction."

"So, what's the answer?" wheezed Don as the threesome began their final lap.

"Once you've inspired – or have been inspired – if you do not know what to do next, take the initiative to ask for direction or look for the next move on your own. A good leader will make it easy for his or her team to take the next step in the process of moving to the Next Level. If the leader fails to do so, it's your responsibility to take the next step on your own – whether that's taking a course, asking for a new experience or finding a mentor to help you make that next step on your own."

"Makes sense," said Randy as they finished the last lap. Michael smiled as both men put their heads down to catch their breaths. After taking a few minutes to recover, Randy noticed Michael had not gone into oxygen debt during their two-mile run. "How did you do that?"

"I'll attribute it to conditioning and getting in about 25 miles of training runs every week," Michael said. "Don't worry. You'll get there. It just takes knowing the next step in your training process."

After rehydrating themselves with some cool water, Michael suggested they walk another few laps to cool down and prevent the lactic acid generated by jogging from causing muscle cramps.

"I'm beginning to figure out going to the Next Level with my running is going to take more than just not wanting to embarrass myself at the next corporate challenge," Randy said. "It's going to take some time … not to mention some real work."

Michael nodded, noting his students were quick to catch on. "Reaching the Next Level, however you define it, doesn't just happen. It takes vision, discipline and action, but taking steps toward systemic change can be the most powerful aspect of this process."

"Not too long ago," Don said, wiping the perspiration from his forehead with a towel as he worked to keep up with the other two men, "corporate challenges were not as competitive. Sometimes people just had to show up to win. Now, with more people involved in competitions, a reasonably good athlete who wants to excel needs a competitive edge. That's the vision, discipline and action you're talking about. Man, do I have a long way to go."

"Maybe not as far as you think" Michael said, reassuringly. "John Wooden, the most successful college basketball coach of all time, and Vince Lombardi, one of the greatest football coaches of all time, both had the same philosophy, 'We master the basics. Then, we drill over and over again on the fundamentals.' The same applies in you reaching your personal and professional Next Levels.

"It's really that simple. Once you know the process for reaching the Next Level successfully, master the basics and then drill on the fundamentals – vision, discipline and action – you'll be ahead of the game."

Now it was Randy's turn. "While we were doing laps, I thought of a question but was too winded to ask. Now that I've had time to catch my breath, I remember the question. Doesn't reaching the Next Level require a certain amount of talent? … I'll use running as an example.

"Some people are just naturally more athletically gifted than others. I know in high school, some of the athletes just seemed to have what it took to be good. Others really had to work … so how does talent factor in when you want to reach the Next Level?"

Michael thought for a moment before answering. "No question, talent is a major part of the equation. I know a lot of talented people who reach a certain level and then start to lose ground. So, what turns the potential of talent into the reality of performance? Some of the words you have heard today and probably words you have heard from your coaches. Those words are: focus, discipline, commitment and action – but most of all endurance."

By this time, the men had completed their cool down, picked up their gym bags and were walking toward the parking lot.

"This has been good," Don said, still perspiring. "I appreciate the workout."

"Me too," Randy echoed. "I don't see my performance reaching the Next Level any time soon, but I'm willing to put in the work."

"Good deal," Michael answered as he opened his car door. "But, before you leave, I have an assignment. At our next meeting, I want you to think about the Next Level you want to achieve. Then, just take me through the steps of what you're going to do to reach that Next Level – from setting the goal and evaluating to what you plan to do when you reach your goal."

The two men nodded. "That'll be a good exercise for me," Randy said. "Sometimes I set goals and then don't think about the tools I'll need to get there."

"We all do that," Michael said, "… and I'll be the first to admit that I've done it. In the meantime, just keep the vision."

STEPPING UP TO THE CHALLENGE – SUMMARY

1. The Next Level – in anything – is more than one element of performance. It's the big picture.

2. To move to the Next Level you must:

   ✦ Set your goal

   ✦ Evaluate the situation

   ✦ Equip yourself

   ✦ Endure while improving

   ✦ Reevaluate performance

   ✦ Evacuate comfort zones

   ✦ Stick to your strategy

   ✦ Set your new goal

3. Taking a step back is sometimes necessary before moving up to the Next Level.

4. Getting to the Next Level doesn't just happen. It takes vision, discipline and action, but taking steps toward systemic change can be the most powerful aspect of this process.

8 Set Your New Goal

7 Stick to Your Strategy

6 Evacuate Comfort Zones

5 Reevaluate Performance

4 Endure While Improving

3 Equip Yourself

2 Evaluate the Situation

1 Set Your Goal

1 SET YOUR GOAL:

Stretch Objectives

> *"The greater danger for most of us lies not in setting our aim too high and falling short, but in setting our aim too low, and achieving our mark."*
> – Michelangelo

When the three men met for their second workout session, Michael's first question was how they felt after their first two-mile run.

"Man, I was so sore the next morning, it took me a few minutes to get out of bed," Randy confessed. "I set up a workout schedule so I ran two miles every other day and by the end of the first week, the soreness had disappeared."

"Great. That means you've conditioned those muscles to withstand a little more stress than they're used to," Michael said. "That's progress."

"I kept thinking about the phrase, 'No pain, no gain,'" Don offered. "I'm taking an ibuprofen each evening I work out, and that helps keep the soreness to a minimum. I'm trying to get in two miles three times a week … and it's getting better. I may add another half mile to my workouts next week."

"Let me warn you. Just when it seems like it's getting easier, adding mileage may be exactly the wrong thing to do," Michael pointed out. "If you're running two miles and you add a half mile, it may not sound like much, but you're actually increasing your run by a quarter of the total distance. That's a lot when you're only in your second week of training."

Don looked puzzled. "But, I thought more mileage would increase my conditioning and help me get faster?"

"Too much of an increase too soon may cause your workouts to become painful again … painful enough to encourage you to skip a run … or two. Then, you're back where you started," Michael counseled. "Let's be realistic. Nobody likes pain … in fact, if you know it's going to hurt, you probably will do whatever it takes to avoid pain. No, Don. I'd suggest you maintain the distance you're running now for at least two more weeks before increasing. That will give your body plenty of time to acclimate, and it will give you a chance to recover well enough so you won't end up on the sofa for the weekend."

"I hear what you're saying," Randy said. "I have a friend who ran cross country in college, and when I asked him about how it felt to run six or eight miles during his training, he explained it by saying, 'It hurts up to a point and then it doesn't get any worse.' I guess that meant his body became accustomed to the distance and the regular runs."

"Exactly. It's a progression that involves small steps," Michael agreed, "but it also requires balance … and by that I mean you don't move your run times to the Next Level by simply getting out and training three or four times a week. Optimally, you'll want to only go up 10 to 15 percent in your mileage and maintain that mileage for about three weeks before changing it again.

"Remember. Once you set your goal, your next steps are to evaluate your current situation and equip yourself to reach the Next Level."

The men nodded.

"Which brings me to your assignment from last week," Michael said. "Do you remember?"

"I even wrote down my response to your question," smiled Randy, pulling a sheet of paper out of his gym bag. "Right now, I'm assistant manager of customer service. My next and most logical move is to customer service manager, but that's probably a year or more away. I figured that out during the second step – evaluation of my current situation. To get there, I need to work on my written communication skills, so I'm taking a course in business communications. That's step three – equipping myself … and I've also requested a chance to go to a few industry seminars, and I am reading a book on customer service management.

"Right now, I'm in the endurance phase, the fourth step. As I take on more responsibilities to find out exactly what I would have to do in the manager's position, it does take endurance," he concluded.

"Great," Michael said, "… and you're right, Randy. Reaching the Next Level does take endurance and commitment to go to seminars and read books, but then you have to come back and start using what you've learned or you forget it. I also admire your initiative in taking on more projects, just to get a feel for the Next Level. Let me know how you're progressing as you go along."

Randy nodded.

"My turn?" Don asked.

"Go for it," said his mentor.

"When I was promoted to team leader two years ago, I determined my team would outperform, outshine and generally dominate in our area," Don began. "I started out by hiring some really talented people and spending a lot of quality time training the group. My first priority was moving the entire team to the Next Level, but I'll be the first to admit … it's slow going. While we've made strides from time to time, we're nowhere near where I thought we would be."

"So, what are you doing in the meantime?" Michael wanted to know.

"In the meantime? Well, I guess I'm feeling sorry for myself because I can't seem to find the answers … the right combination to open the treasure chest," the younger man admitted. "I've attended more than a few leadership conferences and came away with some good ideas, but by the time I get back to the office the next Monday, I'm so overwhelmed with fighting fires and catching up, those great ideas get put on the back burner … well, you know the drill."

"We've all been there," Michael said, "so what can you do differently?"

"Well, I think I have been leading my team about the same way I

3 Easy Ways to Order Copies for Your Management Team!

1. Complete the order form on back and fax to 972-274-2884

2. Visit www.CornerStoneLeadership.com

3. Call 1-888-789-LEAD (5323)

The Next Level ... Leading Beyond the Status Quo provides insight and direction on what it takes to lead your team to a higher and greater Next Level. **$14.95**

Power Exchange – How to Boost Accountability & Performance in Today's Workforce offers practical strategies to help any leader boost accountability and performance in today's workforce. **$9.95**

Monday Morning Communications provides workable strategies to solving serious communications challenges. **$14.95**

Passionate Performance ... Engaging Minds and Hearts to Conquer the Competition offers practical strategies to engage the minds and heart of your team at home, work, church or community. Read it and conquer your competition! **$9.95**

180 Ways to Walk the Recognition Talk will help you provide recognition to your people more often and more effectively. **$9.95**

I Quit, But Forgot to Tell You provides the straightforward, logical truths that lead to disengagement ... and provides the antidotes to prevent the virus from spreading within your organization. **$14.95**

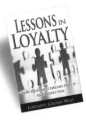

Lessons in Loyalty takes you inside Southwest Airlines to discover what makes it so different ... and successful. **$14.95**

The Manager's Coaching Handbook is a practical guide to improve performance from your superstars, middle stars and falling stars. **$9.95**

Visit www.CornerStoneLeadership.com for additional books and resources.

Start Right – Stay Right is every employee's straighttalk guide to personal responsibility and job success. Perfect for every employee at every level. **$9.95**

The M **Comm** **Handbo** you to c employee the under support a acceptance to your suc **$9.95**

Ouch! that Stereotype Hurts is a guide to show you how to present information and lead discussions in ways that include everyone and avoid bias, stereotyping, or potential discrimination. **$12.95**

The NEW Corne **Perpetual Calen** compelling collec of quotes about leadership and life is perfect for office desks, school and home countertops. Offering a daily dose of inspiration, this terrific calendar makes the perfect gift or motivational reward. **$14.95**

The CornerStone Leadership Collection of Cards is designed to make it easy for you to show appreciation for your team, clients and friends. The awesome photography and your personal message written inside will create a lasting impact. Pack/12 (12 styles/1 each) **$24.95**

Posters also available.

One of each of the items shown here are included in the Accelerate Team Performance Package!

Order Form

_copies $13.95   100+ copies $12.95

_____ copies X _____ = $ _____

...es

(...dable)   _____ copies X $99.95   = $ _____

                            _____ pack(s) X $49.95   = $ _____

... (Pk/20)   _____ pack(s) X $59.95   = $ _____

                            _____ pack(s) X $19.95   = $ _____

...einforcement Kit   _____ kit(s) X $19.95   = $ _____
_Next Level, Reminder
...ational Quote)_

...rformance Resources

...rformance Package   _____ pack(s) X $149.95   = $ _____
(...n of all items shown inside.)

_____   _____ copies X _____   = $ _____

_____   _____ copies X _____   = $ _____

_____   _____ copies X _____   = $ _____

                            Shipping & Handling $ _____

                            Subtotal $ _____

                            Sales Tax (8.25%-TX Only) $ _____

                            Total (U.S. Dollars Only) $ _____

Shipping and Handling Charges

Total $ Amount	Up to $49	$50-$99	$100-$249	$250-$1199	$1200-$2999	$3000+
Charge	$6	$9	$16	$30	$80	$125

Name _____ Job Title _____

Organization _____ Phone _____

Shipping Address _____ Fax _____

Billing Address _____ Email _____
(required when ordering PowerPoint® Presentation)

City _____ State _____ ZIP _____

❏ Please invoice (Orders over $200) Purchase Order Number (if applicable) _____

Charge Your Order: ❏ MasterCard   ❏ Visa   ❏ American Express

Credit Card Number _____ Exp. Date _____

Signature _____

❏ Check Enclosed (Payable to: CornerStone Leadership)

Fax 972.274.2884   www.**CornerStoneLeadership**.com   **P.O. Box 764087**
Phone 888.789.5323   **Dallas, TX 75376**

was training for the 5K. I wanted to reach the Next Level, but I really didn't have a plan. My team is missing what they need most from me ... focus and direction ... a plan. In my eagerness to have the greatest team in the history of the company, I forgot to take time for us to set our team goals and then maintain focus on those goals. I've been frustrated by the lack of improvement – and that's been painful – but I'll also admit, I haven't been crystal clear on what to improve.

"So, this week we had a team meeting, and I asked them the same questions you asked us – what is our Next Level and are we willing to pay the price to reach that level? Much to my amazement, their perception of the Next Level was higher and greater than mine. I had to bring them to reality before we agreed on our next steps. I even used your analogy of the big picture, too much pain and no gain, and how sometimes we have to step back before we step up.

"What we really need to do is get back to the basics.

"That is how we left the meeting. Everyone is to come back this week, evaluate our priorities and develop a plan for us to maintain focus on the priorities of our department.

"And, I came to the realization that I have to maintain my focus – and sometimes get out of the way – so they can get their jobs done."

"I'm impressed with your first assignment," Michael admitted. "You both seem to have some good ideas about what it takes to reach the Next Level – you, Randy, in your job and Don, in your leadership role. So, now let's see how you reach the Next Level in your running.

"Think back to our first workout, while we were running laps," he suggested. "As you ran, you probably evaluated your performance, right?"

They nodded again. "I learned a two-mile run about wiped me out," Randy volunteered. "That's why I decided to run during the week."

"The pain, my friends, is natural as you work toward your goals," Michael affirmed. "Taking steps toward improvement can be the most painful and powerful aspect of any change.

"But during our first run, I also did some evaluating on my own and here's what I saw. Both of you need to go to the gym and do some weight training. I would imagine if you increased both your upper body strength as well as your leg strength, you could probably run a little more efficiently because the additional power would propel you more easily down the track."

"Sounds good," Don said eagerly. "I liked weight training when I was in high school. Just got out of the practice of going to the gym when I went off to college and had to watch my pennies."

"It would take some effort, but you're the coach," Randy said. "I probably need to firm up, as well."

"Glad you brought that up," Michael continued. "I'd like to see both of you adjust your diets and lower your fat intake. You're not too far gone, but you both have some firming up to do."

"Wow. There's more to moving to the Next Level in our running than I thought," Don announced. "I thought I could just get out and run and I would automatically get faster."

"It's all about balance," Michael said. "Your regular running workouts are definitely key, but so is weight training and diet, not to mention being relaxed while you're running and keeping well hydrated … and we've not even gotten into racing strategies yet."

"Say more about balance," Randy requested as he put on his socks and his running shoes.

"I'll tell you a little story," Michael offered. "When I was eight, my mother had my little brother that summer, so I spent a lot of time playing outside and riding my bike. Our house was at the top of a hill … a steep hill, and at the bottom of that hill, the street made a sharp left turn.

"One morning, with the wind behind me, I coasted down the hill. As I gained more speed, I got this wonderful feeling … almost like I was flying. It was a good feeling, going that fast, expending almost no effort at all.

"I was feeling so good … as I came to the sharp corner, I decided not to put on my brakes but, instead, try to maintain that feeling of flying as I rounded the sharp corner. Needless to say, my adrenaline rush ended abruptly as I flew over the handlebars and into the gravel driveway of the house on the corner.

"As you might imagine, I was a mess. My knees and elbows were bleeding and my bike, which was relatively new, was bunged up pretty badly too. I was lucky I hadn't bashed in my skull or broken my neck – and that was the price I paid for being unwilling to give up that feeling of flying in order to maintain my balance while making the sharp turn. On that day, I learned that maintaining your balance is more important than any feeling, any feat or any adrenaline rush you can name."

The two listeners were silent.

"You guys have probably had similar experiences – and you learned that as we negotiate this winding road called life, we continually have to make sacrifices in different parts of our lives," Michael said. "I'm telling you this story to reinforce another point. Balance is everything."

"You mean, not just training with two-mile runs but weight training, diet and lowering our fat intake?" Randy asked rhetorically. "It makes sense. Balance is everything."

Michael nodded. "Balance in training means not running too many miles at a time, running too many times a week, eating too little, working out with weights too much. It means preparing to move to the Next Level but keeping all the plates spinning at one time."

The men nodded.

"Okay. Let's warm-up, and today while you're running, I'd like you to take a look at your running form. Be aware of how you're holding your head, what your arms and hands are doing and how you're putting your foot down and picking it up for the next step."

After stretching and moving to the track, Randy had a question as they began their eight-lap jog. "I understand the importance of warming up when you're working to reach the Next Level, but let's say I want to apply this whole running analogy to moving to the Next Level in my job. What would the warm-up phase be for me?"

"Good question," Michael said as they rounded the first quarter-mile turn. "The warm-up prepares the muscles to perform their best," he explained. "It's also a chance for the brain to send a 'heads up' to the rest of the body, letting all the systems know there's something more than normal activity ahead.

"As far as 'warming up' to move to the Next Level in your job, the exercise is much the same. If you've been strengthening your skills and 'pursuing well-rounded experiences, not to mention volunteering for additional projects, reading books or taking the lead in certain initiatives, you've been warming up for something more than normal activity."

Randy nodded. "Got it, but let's say – and this is just a hypothetical – I have an immediate supervisor who hasn't noticed my 'warm-ups' or who wants me to stay where I am in his organization. Then, what are my chances of moving to the Next Level, even when I've gone through all the steps?"

"Okay, let me see if I can explain this so it makes sense," Michael began. "When you set your goal to move to the Next Level, one of the tasks that goes into meeting that goal is creating the environment to make it possible for that move to happen. Even then, however, the move up is not guaranteed."

His two students looked surprised.

"But then, you know nothing in life is guaranteed, right?"

"Yeah," Randy said after some hesitation.

"Your pause says a lot," Michael smiled as they began their second lap. "Let's suppose your goal is to be a senior sales representative and you are working to make that happen. However, what if your supervisor thinks you'd be more valuable as an analyst or if, unknown to you, another supervisor has voiced an interest in offering you a better opportunity in a totally different department?"

"I see what you're saying," Don chimed in. "Sometimes the Next Level isn't always obvious."

"We can't know everything," Michael agreed. "But, the common thread in all of our scenarios is that you were preparing. You were equipping yourself for greater or different responsibilities and, perhaps, a higher level of performance."

"Just like our workouts now," Randy pointed out. "We've both set our goals. We want to shave some time off our pace, but who knows where we'll be at the next challenge. We may be a little better or a lot better, or we may be doing triathlons. In the interim, nothing is going to change unless we take the steps – like going to the gym and working out – and make the commitment to improve our pace."

At the half-way mark of their run, both of the novices appeared to have much more stamina than at that same point during their first run together. "Well done," said Michael as they began their fifth lap. "You guys aren't breathing nearly as hard or as deeply as you did during our last run. Those workouts during the week are really paying off, but a requirement for success is to keep improving even while you are making significant strides toward your goal. And, as you might guess, I have a story that reinforces my point."

Both younger men were obviously pleased with their individual progress. "Okay, Michael. Tell us your story," Randy said. "We're listening."

"It goes like this," Michael began. "More than 2,000 years ago, a young Greek artist named Timanthes studied under a respected tutor. After working several years, Timanthes painted an exquisite work of art. Unfortunately, he became so enraptured with the painting, he spent days gazing at it without so much as lifting a paintbrush.

"One morning when he arrived to admire his work, he was shocked to find it blotted out with paint. Angry, Timanthes ran to his teacher, who admitted he had destroyed the painting. 'I did it for your own good. That painting was retarding your progress. Start again and see if you can do better.'

"Timanthes took his teacher's advice and went on to produce 'Sacrifice of Iphigenia,' which is regarded as one of the finest paintings of antiquity."

Michael looked at the two men running beside him. "So … I'd like to hear your comments."

"Makes me realize that it's going to take me a while to reach my goal … and I shouldn't be too carried away when I start to see improvement," Don said.

"We've got to keep moving, keep working," Randy agreed.

As the three finished the last lap, Michael gave his students plenty of time to catch their breaths and swig some water before beginning their cool down.

"I timed our run today … about seven minutes per mile … which is good since we weren't racing. Really good for jogging," Michael said. "So, let me ask you, what did you observe during the run about how you were running?"

As usual, Randy was the first one ready with a response. "I saw myself moving my arms across my body instead of keeping them parallel," he said. "After watching you, I tried to correct it and when I did, I noticed that my body was less tense. The motion seemed more natural."

"As you practice it, you'll find it gets even easier," Michael said. "Anything else?"

"I didn't get quite as winded," Randy said, "although I ended the run breathing pretty heavily."

"Me too," Don said. "But, not as badly as the first run. I can see a little difference, but the thing I became most aware of was holding my head over instead of up. Once I straightened up, I didn't feel as much tension in my neck and shoulders."

"Posture is important, especially when you're running … and you can find the most comfortable posture for your body simply by running … by experience," Michael pointed out. "Experience has always been an awesome teacher and mentor for me.

"When I took the vice president's job several years ago, my predecessor – Hanna Lively – gave me some advice I use almost every day since I moved into her office.

"I asked what she had found key to her success in leading the company, and she summed it up in two words, 'good decisions.' I thought for a moment and then asked her how she knew which decisions were good decisions? 'Experience' was her answer … and when I asked how I could get experience, she said two more words, 'bad decisions.' Then she added, 'If you want a place in the sun, you have to expect some blisters.'"

"I can relate," Don said. "I have Band-Aids on three toes right now."

"Same here," Randy grimaced, "and I'm just getting started."

"One more thing and then I'll let you guys get back to your Saturday," Michael said. "One of the aspects of moving to the Next Level includes the possibility of having to give up something … and that 'something' differs with every goal and every individual.

"For me, when I started working to move my 5K pace to the Next Level, I realized I would have to give up my addiction to late night TV. I usually train in the mornings, so I needed the extra sleep in order to get up earlier. It wasn't easy, but I was committed to moving to the Next Level. So, after a few false starts, I finally managed to turn the TV off at 10 p.m. and get in bed at a decent hour. It took a lot of discipline because late night TV had been my 'thing' since my college days, but I determined my goal was more important."

"For me, it's going to be giving up desserts," Randy confessed.

"And, for me it's all about breakfast," Don chimed in. "I usually don't eat breakfast … unless you count a cup of coffee and a donut at work as breakfast. Other than that, I don't eat anything … so that's changing. I'm trying to eat some fruit and cereal every day, but I've had to rearrange my morning schedule to make it happen."

"Well, I had a pep talk prepared to emphasize this point," Michael confessed, "but I see it won't be necessary."

"Keep it on the front burner," Don suggested. "I'll probably need it down the road."

"Yeah, giving up something, whether it's food or TV or something else, isn't always easy," Randy pointed out.

"Especially if that something else is of great importance to you – like friendships or giving up a settled lifestyle because you need to transfer to get the experiences you need to move ahead," Michael added.

The men nodded.

"There's going to be a neighborhood 5K in three weeks, and I'd like both of you to join me, just to see where you are and how you're recovering after the high level of exercise."

"Sounds good," the men said in unison.

"Besides, I need to see if I'm any closer to my goals," Randy added.

"Well, remember the old saying, 'Rome wasn't built in a day,'" their mentor pointed out, "but it never hurts to measure where you are at certain points in your training.

"Oh, and one more thing before we end our workout today," Michael said. "In running ... or any other goal that's important to you, as you work to reach the Next Level ... remember, your toughest opponent of all is the one inside your head. For your next assignment, I'd like you to outline some of the opponents you've been facing as you work to reach the Next Level."

"I don't know if we'll have enough time to get through my list in one Saturday," Don grimaced, picking up his gym bag and catching up with the other two men, as they walked to the parking lot.

"See you guys next time ... and remember – keep the vision," said Michael.

SET YOUR GOAL – SUMMARY

1. Getting to the Next Level is about balance – sharpening obvious skills, honing secondary skills and maintaining balance between people skills and professional skills.

2. Taking steps toward the Next Level can be the most painful and also the most powerful aspect of any change.

3. If you want a place in the sun, expect some blisters.

4. Moving to the Next Level includes the possibility of having to give up something ... and that "something" differs with every goal.

2 EVALUATE THE SITUATION:

Who, What, When

"Surround yourself with people who can't live without football,
recognize winners – they come in all forms
and have a plan for everything."
– Legendary Football Coach Bear Bryant

When the three met at the track for their third training session, Michael wanted to know about their experiences at the neighborhood 5K the week before, but he also wanted to hear each of his protégés talk about their last assignment – identifying their opponents as they worked to reach the Next Level.

Again, Randy was first. "As I worked on my list, I came up with some surprises," he began. "I mean, there were the usual roadblocks but there were also some opponents I wasn't expecting."

Michael nodded. "Surprises?"

"Well, okay … my wife, Katie, for example. I mean, she's great. We have a good marriage, a wonderful new baby and we get along really well … we're a team … and we always have been. But, as I'm preparing myself to move to the Next Level, she's having some problems with how I prioritize my time. She understands what I'm doing, but she often wants more of my time than I have to give." Randy explained.

Don nodded in agreement. "I know exactly what you mean. You may have been surprised, but your situation is not unique, especially when there's a new baby in the house. My best friend's wife was completing her residency in medical school several years ago, which required long shifts and being away from home for 24 hours … sometimes more. So, while she was working, my friend frequently had time off – especially on the weekends – so we spent time together. He intellectually understood her need to spend the time away from home, but emotionally he had some real problems with it. When they sat down and discussed why he felt abandoned, they were able to make some adjustments to work through the long periods of being apart without feeling abandoned."

Randy looked grim. "I guess the bottom line is that I'm not balancing my work life and my home life. I know taking care of the baby all day isn't easy and that my wife has made several adjustments. Maybe I'm not collaborating with my wife enough."

"That's not an easy one, especially with a child … and it takes real commitment … from both of you," Don added.

"So, Randy, any more surprises in the way of your opponents?" Michael wanted to know.

"One other big one … me! Like I said, I don't have good time management skills, so I spend too much time getting too little done. That leaves me little time with my wife, little time to train and little time to take care of my spiritual life. Looking back on this year alone, I've spent more Sundays at the office or working on projects at home than I have in church."

"Like we talked about last time, balance is vitally important," Michael emphasized. "It all comes down to the choices we make. If your work life is eating up your time for a home life, you need to work smarter and put your work life on a diet."

Randy looked startled. "A diet?"

Michael explained, "By that I mean, giving yourself manageable and reasonable goals and focusing on meeting them within the time frame you allow yourself. You will find that with better prioritization and organization you can get more done in less time. There are plenty of books available on the subject … may be worth your investment."

Randy looked a little less concerned. "You are right. I need to take control of my own time. I'm going to buy a time management book this weekend and start attacking my obstacle. That's about all for me, but the opponents I identified will keep me busy for a while," Randy said, almost apologetically.

"You're up next," Michael said, turning to Don.

"I'll make this brief," Don said, "because I know we all want to get on the track before it gets too warm. Anyway, I identified four opponents keeping me and my team from getting to the Next Level."

"We're ready to hear them," Michael said, "but take your time."

"Okay … here they are. Number one is other departments – they don't understand what we're trying to do. Second is confusion, followed closely by time and lastly, people on the team who don't want what I want," Don said, folding the list he was reading from.

"Well, that's definitely brief, but aside from identifying these opponents, tell us what you're doing about them," Michael coached, "and by the way, I have seen the same opponents in various phases of my own career, just as I have experienced some of the surprise opponents Randy identified … so, let's begin with other departments. What are you doing to disarm those opponents?"

"Here's what's going on, so far. There are people from other departments who don't understand what we're trying to do in elevating our team to the Next Level. So, we're putting together a communications process so other departments we work with will understand what we're doing and exactly how it impacts what they do. That process will include more interdepartmental meetings, so we can understand what they're doing and how it impacts us," Don reported.

"That's a great starting point … and your communications process will be invaluable when change occurs," Michael commented.

"Next, in trying to deal with the confusion that often gets in our way, we discussed this within our team and it came up that when we've instituted change in the past, not everyone could get on board until we honed our focus and plotted our direction," Don continued. "As a team, we've identified our focus, and as team leader, it's my job to eliminate elements that are not helping us achieve our goals. I haven't done such a hot job in that area in the past, so it's going to be a challenge, but I think I am up to it."

"Sounds like a good strategy," Michael nodded. "You're giving the team ownership of the goals you all have set. Let me illustrate it with something I noticed during my travels … and I know you travel a lot, so you must also rent cars when you travel, right?"

"They know me almost by name at the car rental agency," Don laughed.

"So, tell me … how many times have you washed a rental car?" asked Michael.

"Well, I don't think I've ever washed one," Don admitted.

"That's my point. If you don't own it, you treat the car differently. Me, I've never even thought about washing a rental car, even though I wash our cars weekly … and vacuum them too. It's the same with your team. If they own their goals, they're going to treat them differently than if you set them and just handed them over."

"I hadn't thought of it that way," Don confessed, "but one thing I have learned is that it takes time – formulating plans and preparing ourselves – to meet the Next Level. As I discussed this with our team and then thought about it later, as the team leader, I've never provided time to plan and prepare. Once I realized this, I committed myself to spending more time planning, along with the team. That way, we'll have to spend less time reacting. It makes a lot of sense … at least to me.

Michael smiled and nodded. Don was making some large strides toward the Next Level … in his team leadership as well as his running.

"The last opponents I've found are the people on the team who are perfectly happy with the status quo instead of wanting to improve," Don admitted. "Some of these folks see the light when you give them options. Others have required disciplinary actions, but they also have choices. They can either change and improve with us … or they may be happier working in another department or with another company."

"I must say," Michael said after a few moments, "I'm really impressed with your analysis … and I think these assignments force us to take a look at an issue from all sides. I'm pleased with what both of you discovered – and your remedies … so, let's continue this dialogue down the road … and now I want to hear about the 5K last Saturday."

"Well, I could see the regular runs had made a difference," Don was first to share. "My problem, though, was starting at the front of the pack."

"That was a problem?" Randy wondered.

"Being in front forced me to start at a faster pace than I could sustain for very long," Don explained. "By the end of the first mile, I was sucking air and was out of energy."

"I learned the same lesson," Michael said. "When you start out in front, something happens to your brain and you morph into the late, great Steve Prefontaine – the Olympian who defied rules, pushed limits … and smashed records – and would eventually win the race. That never happened to me. The best I could do was finish the race and end up lying spread-eagle on the track at the finish line."

"I definitely learned a lesson," Don agreed. "From now on, I'll start at the middle ... or even the back of the pack, so I can set my own pace instead of trying to match someone else's."

"What about you, Randy? How was the race for you?"

"Well, I finished ... and my time wasn't bad ... better than the corporate challenge," he began, "but after being pushed and jostled in the middle of the pack, I slowed down so I could just enjoy the run."

"Hmmm. Doesn't sound like either one of you had much fun," Michael observed. "Don't you remember? Running, aside from being good exercise and challenging, has got to be fun or you won't keep it up. It's like the pain thing. If you know you're going to hurt, you're not going to do it. If it's not fun, sooner or later, you're going to give it up."

The two students looked at each other, trying to figure out where Michael was headed.

"Okay. Let's talk about the race this way. Years ago, somebody decided running was a lonely sport ... an individual endeavor," Michael began. "What they didn't think about is that competing requires at least one more person."

"I'll buy that – except I thought we were competing against ourselves, trying to improve the last time we posted?" Randy asked, putting on his running shoes.

"That's part of it, but I'll guarantee if you run a 5K by yourself and then run a 5K with me, your time will be faster when you have somebody to run with, or as the real competitors say, 'against.'

"The runners who make the greatest strides are those who have workout partners, people to work with, people to push them a little harder than they would push themselves, people who they can run with during the big races," Michael pointed out.

"So, how could we have helped each other in last Saturday's race?" Don wanted to know as they began their stretching and warm-up in preparation for today's run.

"First of all, you each know the other's goals – and also about how fast the other runs," Michael began. "You run together often, so you're probably close to the same rhythm and at the same point in your development. By running together, you could have established a manageable pace, not going out too fast to stay ahead of or to keep up with the pack.

"Secondly, a little collaboration would have kept you from being jostled – because the two of you could have created your own space by running together. Finally, by going out together, you would have probably hung in with more energy because you had company and you didn't feel like you were all by yourselves."

"But, we had a lot of people around us," Randy protested.

"Yeah, but have you ever heard the phrase, 'feeling all alone in a crowd?' I'll bet you didn't know the person next to you, and I'll bet you had feelings of being in the middle of nowhere all by yourselves."

The two men nodded.

"Feeling like you're all alone is a bummer," Michael continued, "and when you feel that way, you don't always perform at the top of your game.

"Okay, now apply what I've just shared to your race on Saturday and to your training and you'll immediately see the impact of collaborative effort, both on the track and at the office . Whether the other person helps push you to a faster pace, serves as a drafting partner or simply provides companionship during miles and miles of otherwise singular and lonely effort, a partner will always be more of a benefit than a detriment as you strive to achieve your goal," Michael concluded.

"I'll buy that," Don said, "and I have seen the difference in my training runs during the week – when I run alone – and when we train together. I'm never as tired, maybe because of the conversation, but definitely because the three of us are working together toward a common goal."

"Why shouldn't collaborations be the rule in the workplace?" Michael asked.

"Probably because our performance is rated on our individual contribution," Randy offered.

"My theory is that individuals can't have the same momentum and innovative capacity that teams are able to offer," Michael said. "Maybe we've reached the point where both individual and team performance should be rated."

"You definitely make a good case," Don agreed.

"Well, it's something to think about," Michael said, leading the trio to the track to begin their laps. "Since we've been at this for two months now, let's add two laps to our usual eight?"

"I'm game," Randy said, taking a slight lead over the other two.

As the three jogged around the track, each one took his turn, taking the lead and cutting through the wind resistance so the other two could run easier. At the end of the first mile, Michael suggested they stop and look at their watches.

"Even at our jog pace, we've cut more than 30 seconds off our usual time," Randy said, unable to hide the surprise in his voice. "This collaboration thing is awesome."

Don agreed. "Randy, we're going to have to start doing some of our weekly runs together," he suggested. "This could get us both to our goals in no time at all."

"Now that you've seen what collaboration can do on the track, let's talk about the other 'people' factors you need to reach your goal – because having another person to run with isn't the only consideration," said Michael as the three started their second mile around the track.

"In order to get the best out of your collaborative efforts – both in your running and in the workplace – another consideration is finding the right people to train with," he pointed out. "For a while, my wife, Pam, and I ran together on Saturday mornings. We both enjoyed it … well, we just enjoy being together … period. But, I soon found myself dropping back to match her pace instead of improving my own.

"Nothing against Pam. She's a good runner … and we still run together, but the training benefit comes from running with other runners who are better than I am or about the same.

"Running with someone a little stronger pushes you to pick up your own pace," Michael said, "and when you run with someone at about the same pace, you maintain where you are.

"It's all about collaborating with the right people – and the same is true in business. I'm sure you probably studied some of the old business models in school – where one guy had all the information and then delegated specific duties to the rest of the company. That's a true 'top-down model.'

"Today, we know that teams function better when everyone is up to speed with what everyone else knows about the project. This is what I call the operational business intelligence model, where actionable business information is extended to employees throughout the company. The OBI model provides input and feedback to every level of the corporation, equipping everyone to be at least the same speed with everyone else, depending on their team's objective," Michael explained. "When properly constructed, operational business intelligence systems enable and optimize the performance of the processes necessary to make the team successful."

"So, you're talking about teams of the right people with the right information?" Don wanted to know.

"Think about it this way," Randy suggested as they rounded the far turn to begin their two additional laps. "I watched Lance Armstrong win his seventh Tour de France. Before the race began, Lance's team – The Discovery Channel Team – was pronounced to be the strongest cycling team ever. When I heard that, I understood the strategy. The team's sponsors surrounded the best cyclist in the world – Lance Armstrong – with others cyclists who were all strong and could help him win the seventh Tour."

"So much for the power of one," Don pointed out.

"In fact, every cyclist on the team had to be strong," Michael interjected. "Team Discovery wanted to make sure their star was supported, but in the unlikely event he faltered, they still wanted a shot at the yellow jersey. In this case, it was the power of one multiplied by nine – and it works that way in business too. If you surround yourself with the right people, you can multiply the power of one – and, ultimately, achieve your goal. If you try to go it alone, just like in running, that road gets longer and longer, there's no one to push you, you run out of gas and eventually you hit the wall."

By this time, the three had completed the additional two laps – a half mile more.

"I need to lie down," Randy moaned. "That last quarter mile got me … guess I wasn't ready."

"Keep walking," Michael coached. "You need to get the by-products of oxidation out of your legs and walking helps you recover."

After a two-lap cool down, the men picked up their gear and headed for the parking lot. "What you said about the people part of success makes a lot of sense," Don said as he opened the back of his SUV and put in his running bag. "It's a whole new direction for me. I've practiced self-sufficiency all throughout my career."

"And, that's still not a bad practice," Michael said, "but being a strong contributor and surrounding yourself with strong team members will get you farther faster ... and I just happened to have a story to end our conversation today."

The other two men looked at each other and smiled. "We were waiting."

Michael continued, "Two corporate teams met for a rowing competition. To the consternation of the host company, the rival team immediately moved to the front and won by 11 lengths.

"The management of the host company was embarrassed by its poor showing and promptly appointed a committee to figure out why they lost and make recommendations to improve their team's chances in a rematch the following year. The committee appointed a task force to study the race. They met for three months and issued a preliminary report. In essence, the report said that the rival crew had been unfair.

"They had eight people rowing and one coxswain steering and shouting out the beat. The report said, 'We had one person rowing and eight coxswains.'

"The chairman of the board thanked the committee and sent it away to study the matter further and make recommendations for the rematch. Four months later the committee came back with a recommendation – Our guy has to row faster."

"I get it," Randy said as Don rolled his eyes.

"It's something to think about," Michael said. "In fact, I'd like you to think about the idea of collaboration as it applies to your personal or business goals and bring back your thoughts when we meet again."

His two students nodded.

"That'll be easy," Don waved.

EVALUATE THE SITUATION – SUMMARY

1. Identify opponents preventing you from reaching the Next Level … and then develop remedies.

2. Identify goals and strategize focus. Those team members satisfied with status quo should be (a) brought up to speed or (b) encouraged to transfer.

3. Teach the business of the business by exploiting operational business intelligence and achieving teams of the right people with the right information.

4. Multiply the power of one by the number of strong members on your team.

3 EQUIP YOURSELF:

Duck and (Re)Cover

"If you watch how nature deals with adversity, continually renewing itself and becoming stronger, you can't help but learn."
– Bernie Siegel, M.D., pediatrician and author

As Don and Randy joined Michael for their fourth training session, they all realized it wasn't going to be easy that day. Even the early morning sun was more searing than any of their other Saturday meetings.

"I want to save discussion of our assignment for the end of the workout and get started before it gets too hot," Michael began.

"How hot was it supposed to get today? Anybody know?" Don asked as they finished their warm-up stretching and were well into their first lap around the track.

"Don't know," Randy responded. "It's been in the high 90s every day this week … and look … not a cloud in the sky."

"The thing about training," Michael pointed out, "is that it is an everyday thing, especially if you're totally committed to your goal … and I want you guys to start thinking about a more regular training schedule. It's time to move your efforts to the Next Level, which means a fairly rigid schedule."

"You mean three runs a week and our monthly Saturday meetings aren't enough?" asked Randy.

"If you're serious about moving your times to the goals you set, you'll have to pay the price," Michael said.

"A regular training schedule will help you increase your efficiency as well as get faster because it emphasizes developing cardio-respiratory endurance. And, it will also help you condition your mental focus so that you have the discipline to equip yourself for The Next Level. But, always remember … Rome wasn't built in a day."

The two men nodded. "We're finding that out."

As they completed their first mile, Don suddenly stopped running. "Man, I've got to stop. I'm not feeling so hot … in fact, I'm really hurting."

Michael walked back to check on his student, who was now sitting on the track, doubled over with cramps. "Well, we're definitely in the heat today," he began, "and I'm wondering how much hydrating you did before getting here this morning."

"Not much, I'm afraid," Don admitted.

"Just to be on the safe side, why don't you sit out the next mile in the shade – and start sipping some Gatorade," their mentor suggested. "One of my cardinal rules is listen to your body and don't push it."

Once Don was safely in the shade with a dampened a towel to put over his head and was rehydrating, Michael and Randy went back to the track to finish their run. "That's scary," Randy observed. "What if that had happened during a race?"

"One of the things I've learned over my years of training is how to recover from the unexpected," Michael said. "By the time you've been running as long as I have, you gain a sixth sense about your body and how it's responding. During one of my runs, I began feeling sort of woozy and stopped in a shady spot to regain my bearings. It was hot that day and I had just gotten over a bout of the stomach virus, so I definitely was not my best. It happened when I was training with my coach, so I wasn't alone, which was lucky.

"When I had finally cooled off enough to head home, I was feeling terrible, so I went to the doctor that afternoon," Michael continued. "He checked me from head to toe, including a treadmill EKG, and after all the test results came back, the doc told me I apparently had a reaction to the sun. It had never happened before and has never happened since, but I knew enough to stop, cool off and get back home before I got worse."

"So, did that interrupt your training?" Randy asked.

"Only for a couple of weeks," Michael replied, "and when I got back to my regular training schedule, the time off had actually allowed my body to recover enough so I was running more efficiently – and faster – than before.

"Staying as healthy as possible so you can train regularly is a big component in reaching your goal," he continued, "but recovering from unexpected adversity is also an important part of the big picture ... and whether we want to admit it or not, like Don found out today, we're always going to have unexpected adversity. In a way, it's good to even have a plan for what you'll do when adversity occurs."

"The first thing I would do is pray that I won't have any adversity to deal with," Randy said as they began their last half mile.

"That's a good idea too," his mentor said, "but I'll guarantee you, it happens ... even to the best people. I mean, why do you think they're putting those satellite communications devices on more and more new cars?"

"Because people need help at their fingertips?" Randy responded.

"Adversity, whether it's locking yourself out of your car, running out of gas, a flat tire – or worse – happens," Michael said, "and being able to recover from adversity quickly has become very important, mainly because of the speed of our lives."

"Never thought about the speed of life before ... but it makes sense," Randy said, pondering the idea.

"So, as the speed of life increases, the speed of business also accelerates," he continued, "which is why it's important for businesses to be agile enough to recover faster from unexpected adversity."

"Exactly ... business is moving at warp speed these days, but I didn't have to tell you a story in order for you to make the connection," Michael joked. "I must be losing my touch."

"In fact, I have a story," Randy announced. "May I?"

"Be my guest."

"There's this kid named Jeremy that I read about. I think he comes from somewhere around Dayton, Ohio. Anyway, his family had owned a successful manufacturing firm for about 80 years. This kid was 18 and in his first year of college when his stepfather, who was president of the family firm, was accidentally shot and killed during a hunting trip.

"At that point, Jeremy made the decision to drop out of school, and he went to work for the company, sweeping floors and doing whatever was needed to keep the place going while he learned the business," Randy continued. "His grandfather returned from retirement to run the company and coach him, and Jeremy also took some business courses. Two years later, he became president of the corporation.

"He once told a buddy, 'When you're faced with adversity, you have two choices: You can either crawl up in a hole and never recover or you can excel.'

"Jeremy gave up a lot of the 'fun' activities that most college kids enjoy. He chose to make the best of his adversity and excel in the opportunity that was before him. Today, this incredible young man is leading a staff of 20 employees supplying 1,800 distributors around the world."

"Great story," Michael agreed. "His agility, flexibility and ability to recover quickly from adversity made the difference. I've also heard CEOs saying they look for people for their management teams who have those same qualities. Without that resilience and the ability to recover quickly, when a company hits a rough spot in the road, there's a real chance it will fail unless it has that buoyancy you described to survive.

"Speaking of resilience, looks like Don has about overcome his own adversity this morning," said Michael, pointing to a lone runner, jogging across the field.

"Man, that was a surprise," Don said as he began walking with the two men who were now into their cool down. "That's never happened to me before … but tell me, what did I miss?"

"I'll let Randy bring you up to speed … but it's good to see you up and moving again," his mentor offered. "Now that you know how it feels to get dehydrated. …"

"I promise I'll be well-hydrated from now on," the ailing runner allowed. "Have I missed any of Michael's stories?"

"Randy was the storyteller today, but don't worry, I have a story of my own," Michael smiled.

The three men finished their cool down walk and were now sitting in the shade of the track's bleacher section, enjoying some cold Gatorade.

"We've been talking about the ability to recover from unexpected adversity," Michael began, "but there's something else that comes into play when we talk about adversity, and that's having the vision to anticipate any possible problems and then designing processes to avoid them.

"Many years ago, before either of you guys were born, the renowned architect Frank Lloyd Wright was offered the task of building the Imperial Hotel in Tokyo. As recent history has demonstrated, the islands of Japan seem to be ground zero for some horrendous earthquakes, something that Mr. Wright had to take into consideration as he designed the hotel.

"To give you some idea of how formidable this task was, no comparable construction job ever before had been undertaken.

"After spending many months reviewing the situation, he found a 60-foot bed of soft mud lying about eight feet below the surface of downtown Tokyo. The building Wright was asked to design was immense in its size, so the architect decided to 'float' the structure on the bed of mud, which would absorb the shock of any earthquakes or the equally destructive tremors that usually follow.

"It took Wright four years to build the Imperial Hotel in Tokyo, and believe me, he was surrounded by naysayers and skeptics, all sure his idea would fail, but eventually the most difficult building project was completed … and eventually the day arrived when it was tested. Tokyo's worst earthquake in 52 years caused many of Tokyo's buildings and much of its housing to collapse in ruins. However, the Imperial Hotel withstood the test, able to adjust itself to the tremors that shook Tokyo to its core that day as Wright's detractors were silenced.

"Of course, it's difficult to foresee the glitches that could come up," Michael concluded, "but like any vision, contingency planning doesn't hurt and, in many cases, that planning can make a huge difference – as the Imperial Hotel story demonstrates."

The trio sat quietly until Don spoke. "Well, I'll be better prepared for our next run … but I apologize for today."

"Don't give it another thought," Michael reassured. "The most important part is getting back on your feet and getting back on track … as fast as you can. Think of it as being your best at the worst time. So, anyone up to walking to Starbucks for some air conditioned comfort and an iced latte?"

"Sounds too good to pass up," Don agreed eagerly.

"Me too," Randy said.

"Great, because I want to ask you guys a few questions before I let you go today," said Michael, leading the way.

Once they had settled themselves in the comfortable chairs around the table, Michael was ready with his questions. "At the end of our last workout, I asked you to think about collaborations that have made a difference in your efforts to reach the Next Level."

Don, now fully recovered from his earlier episode of dehydration, went first. "I've worked with teams my entire career, but I hadn't thought much about collaborations because we were always working to meet assigned quotas, so it was pretty much everyone for themselves. But, I'd like to share some things I learned after holding a strictly voluntary meeting last month.

"I invited the team to an after-hours meeting led by our CFO. I asked him if he would mind conducting a workshop on the business of our business. The CFO was thrilled that I asked and much to my surprise every member of the team showed up.

"Wow! Was I ever elated ... and pleased. The neat thing is that I discovered that the more my team knew about how our organization pays the bills, the better the decisions my team made. By sharing information from the CFO, we were all able to be on the same page.

"That was a big 'Aha!' for me ... but even more importantly, I started to see that the team really wanted to make the organization better when they understood what to do and why it was important. Until they had the right information, they didn't know how to make all the pieces fit together, so I'm trying to do a better job in making sure they have as much information as is available," Don said.

"It is amazing ... and making sure everybody has the right information can definitely make a difference," Michael agreed. "By having the meeting with the CFO, you were offering the team members a chance to identify, to belong to the organization ... in a way, the information made them true stakeholders in the organization's future. You helped them accept ownership for your team instead of just renting time at work. That is terrific."

Now, it was Randy's turn. "My example is not nearly as dramatic as Don's, but it is one that has really made a difference in my journey recently. Remember last time we were together, I told you I was surprised that my wife was an opponent of sorts as I was working my way to the Next Level?

"Well, after Michael mentioned collaborations that were important, I decided I hadn't made much effort to make Katie my collaborator and a part of my team, so I began working on that. After all, whatever career successes I have directly affect the lifestyle I can provide for Katie and the baby. I began sharing more information with Katie about the demands on my time, the goals I was pursuing and how I was feeling about my progress."

"And, what was the result?" asked Michael.

"The result was a stronger collaboration. Katie began to realize she was a part of Team Randy … and that I was part of Team Katie, as well. We began organizing our time better, figuring out when we could share our downtime and how we could help the other with the bigger jobs. It has made a difference!"

Michael smiled. "That's why lifeboats are big enough for several people, not just one. Getting through adversity, achieving goals or simply improving your race time is always more fun – and more gratifying – when you can share the accomplishment with someone else … or an entire team. Of course, having collaborations on the heavy lifting also means you not only get through it but you get through it faster. Plus you have someone to celebrate with at the end."

He held up his coffee cup. "A toast, gentlemen – to collaborations and the valuable place they occupy in equipping ourselves to reach the Next Level."

"Hear, hear," Don agreed.

"Speaking of collaborations," Randy said, "I need to get going. Katie has an appointment in 30 minutes, and I promised to take care of our baby while she had some time away from our little darling."

"I've got chores too," Michael said as they walked toward the parking lot. "In the meantime, keep your goals in mind … and keep the vision."

EQUIP YOURSELF – SUMMARY

1. Equipping for the Next Level means being able to recover from unexpected adversity.

2. Create a contingency plan on how you will react to an unexpected crisis.

3. Understanding the "business of your business" creates ownership for your team members.

4. Collaborations are important for accomplishing goals and celebrating the achievement.

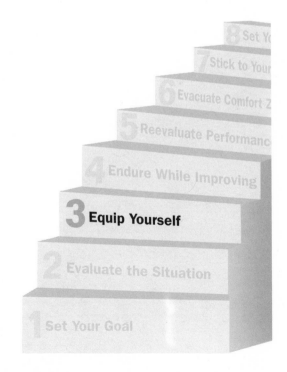

4 ENDURE WHILE IMPROVING:

Courage to Change

*"It takes courage to release the familiar, to embrace the new.
In change there is power."*
– Alan Cohen, author of "Chicken Soup for the Soul"

As Michael drove into the track's parking lot, he glimpsed at his two students already warming up. It was a good sign, he decided, considering they could easily be burning out at this point in their training.

"How is your new workout schedule coming along?" was Michael's first question.

"Actually, I think the new schedule, which gives me some time to recover, is much better than what I was doing before," Randy said, enthusiastically.

"Same here," said Don. "I see progress – serious progress, which is terrific! Before, I was inconsistent in my training and seemed to be running in place … if you'll pardon the pun."

"No problem," Michael laughed, "but today I want you to make some more of that serious progress. Let's start off our workout today with Newton's third law."

"Well, what if I'm not sure about Newton's first law … ?" Randy chuckled.

"Won't take long to get you up to speed," Michael reassured, "but this particular law has to do with your running style, and according to Mr. Newton, 'for every action, there is an equal and opposite reaction.' If we apply that to running, the most effective running style would be to go straight down the track in one giant step. Unfortunately, to reach the end of the track, we have to take several steps – so, to get there efficiently, we want all motions to aim straight ahead. The equal and opposite would be straight back."

"You've lost me," Don admitted.

"Okay. Let me put it this way. You don't want any sideways motions, so if your right arm flails out instead of moving straight ahead, the equal and opposite action will also be sideways, which will keep you from moving ahead as quickly. So, let's say when you're running, your right arm goes sideways – and that means your right foot will go out to the side too. If you're not running efficiently, it takes more energy to get to the finish line," Michael explained. "The less energy you use, the faster you'll be able to run.

"I've noticed that both of you bring your arms up and across your bodies when you run," Michael continued. "I was doing the same thing when I started running several years ago. By correcting that one motion – from sideways to straight forward and straight back, you'll pick up speed and probably won't be as tired after a long run."

"Sounds easy," Randy observed, standing and moving his arms to simulate Michael's example.

"One more thing, Randy. When you're running, you only want to use the muscles you need, no more – no less," Michael pointed out. "See how you're clinching your fists?"

Randy looked at his hands. Sure enough, his fists were tightly clinched.

"If you clinch your fists while you're running, you're also flexing the muscles in your hands and arms, and that takes oxygen – oxygen you could be using in your legs, instead," Michael explained. "Relaxing your hands means they require less oxygen, leaving that energy to go into your legs."

Don was on his feet now, moving his arms and keeping his hands relaxed. "I think I see what you mean."

"Okay, so let's move onto the track and get started," said Michael.

After the three had taken a slow jog around the first lap, Michael asked them to pick up the pace, using the new techniques he had demonstrated earlier. As the three ran the next lap, Michael paid close attention to their facial expressions.

"Let's slow the pace so we can discuss one more change," Michael said. "Remember how I said you should only use the muscles necessary for running?"

The two men nodded, still trying to catch their breaths from the last lap.

"The same thing applies to your face. If you run with your mouths closed and your jaws clinched, you're using more muscles than you need," explained their mentor. "You've seen world-class sprinters come down the tracks with their jaws loose or even flopping?"

His students nodded again.

"They've learned to run with a loose, relaxed jaw, allowing the oxygen needed for keeping the mouth closed and the jaw clinched to go to their legs, where the real energy is needed.

"So, if you're clinching your jaws, or any other muscles not needed for running, you'll need to work on changing your style. Keep your bodies relaxed. Keep your hands cupped, your jaw loose and allow the rest of your energy to concentrate on picking up and putting down your feet. Oh, and don't forget Newton's third law."

"Wow! I never thought there was a science to relaxing," Don said.

"Making these changes now, as difficult as it may seem, is much easier than making them later on," Michael explained. "Okay, let's take a slower lap so you can start incorporating some of these suggestions in your running styles."

Over the course of the next hour, the two younger men stopped and started their trips around the track, focusing on the changes their mentor had recommended, but – at times – becoming frustrated with the difficulty they were having in making the energy-saving changes.

Once they had concluded their usual 10-lap workout, Michael gave his students an opportunity to moan and groan about changing their running styles. "Obviously, you know what you're talking about," Randy concluded, "but it's darned hard to change once you've been doing it the same way for awhile."

"Exactly," Michael said, "and I had to go through the same frustrations you've had today. If you really want to change your running style – to make it more efficient – it'll take a week or two before you'll see any benefits … but, I can guarantee, you'll be glad you made the changes."

"I didn't realize it was going to be so painful," Randy admitted.

"Remember the old saying, 'No pain – no gain?'" Don asked.

"Well, while we're doing our cool down, guess what?" Michael wanted to know.

"You've got a story?" Don responded haltingly.

"Ever heard of Levi Strauss?"

"Who hasn't – I mean, he started the whole thing about jeans, didn't he?"

"Right … but he developed his jeans by sheer accident," Michael continued. "He was the son of a tailor who decided to seek his fortunes during the California gold rush. However, he soon learned that available clothing wasn't made sturdy enough to stand the wear and tear of mining for gold, so he abandoned his mining pursuits and eventually found a serge fabric from Nimes, France (called 'serge de Nimes' – which eventually formed the word 'denim') and started making work clothes for the swarms of miners working in the area.

"To reinforce the seams of his workpants – so they would stand up to the rigors of mining – Strauss started using copper rivets to make sure the seams wouldn't tear out, even after hard use.

"Needless to say, his denim jeans were popular, and eventually, not only miners were buying them, but also others involved in the more physical professions like ranch workers and cowboys.

"Leap ahead 20 years to the 1870s, where cowboys wearing dusty Levi's are gathered around a blazing campfire after a long day in the saddle. Suddenly one of the cowboys lets out a yelp and stumbles back from the fire – yet another victim of 'Hot Rivet Syndrome.'

"Strauss, in his original design (what we know as the Levi's 501), used the copper rivets to reinforce the inseams and when cowboys crouched too long and too close to the campfire, those rivets grew uncomfortably hot.

"For years, those brave cowboys suffered this unusual occupational hazard. Then, in 1933, Levi Strauss President Walter Haas went camping, wearing his 501s into the High Sierras. Crouching by a blazing campfire, drinking in the invigorating night air, Haas suddenly experienced 'Hot Rivet Syndrome.'

"Consulting with the professional wranglers in his group, Haas found they, too, had suffered from the same mishap, so when he returned home after the trip, he met with the Levi Strauss board of directors and on his recommendation, the offending rivets were voted into extinction.

"Change is always painful – for someone," Michael concluded with a chuckle, "but it is always possible. Sometimes it just takes the right person to recognize the need for change. ..."

"Or the right person experiencing the right pain," Randy added.

"Even if you're dominating the market, change will pay dividends," Michael agreed. "I don't know of one business that has perfect processes in every area, even if they're utilizing the latest and greatest technology. By looking at those processes with an eye for finding a more efficient way to reach the same result, renovation sharpens the competitive edge and, for the various stakeholders, becomes the sign of a healthy organization.

"In the case of the Levi's, Haas had a best-selling product with one tiny flaw ... so he reinvented how the jeans were put together," Michael pointed out. "In other situations, organizations and even individuals get to the Next Level by reinventing themselves.

"Take today, for example. In essence, you guys have been reinventing your running styles to make your running more efficient and less energy consuming. Oh, you could have made some progress by maintaining the styles you had and just building your stamina, but by making these changes, by tweaking your style just a little, you're poised to make giant steps in your speed as well as your stamina ...

and it's the same in business. By making changes, sometimes only small ones, it's not always easy because change takes discipline, as you've found, as well as personal commitment and willingness to make the change. But, the improved outcomes are worth the struggle."

"I'm going to be working on it," said Don. "To be honest, I didn't realize I was clenching anything until you pointed it out. Now that I'm aware, I can tell that releasing that tightness in my arms and face is making a difference."

"Think about this for a minute. In companies and other institutions where leadership allows employee autonomy, production increases," Michael pointed out. "Unclenching the fists of stringent rules and allowing operations to run with a slack jaw, so to speak, often feeds more energy and innovation into the organization's employees who, in turn, work harder and innovate more efficient processes."

"Yeah, like you said, by using those unnecessary muscles, it is definitely taking something away," Randy said. "Like a lot of energy I need elsewhere."

"Your comments bring me to my final point for the day. If you think about it, like running with your fists clenched or tight jaws, most businesses do things that are unnecessary … things that are not the most efficient and productive use of energy or resources," Michael said. "In one of my first jobs, we had many meetings that were absolutely unnecessary, but they had always run the business that way. Those meetings took time away from our productivity and, with rare exception, were an absolute waste of time for all of us who were required to attend."

"I hear you. Early on in my career, I also had a boss that wanted us in the office at 7 a.m. every day to eat donuts, drink coffee and generally talk about our plans for the day. If I could have used that same energy to set appointments or to make cold calls, I would have seen a lot more commissions," Don said.

"There are also organizations that, often without knowing it, allow what I call 'stress-producing' activities to go on in an office that literally saps everyone's productivity," Michael said. "Things like negative discussions, 'witch hunts' when someone needs to place the blame for a mistake or even personal vendettas among employees.

"Think about this," he continued. "If you took the time and energy employees use for water fountain gossip and put it into a campaign to develop new customers, you'd have a real winner. No question."

"But, changing is so difficult," Randy reminded.

"It is absolutely difficult to change, no question," Michael agreed, "or maybe I should say, it's difficult at first, and it takes practice to make it part of your culture. But, if you're committed, if you have the vision and if you have goals to reach, those painful changes will, ultimately, take you to the Next Level. Now, before I go, I have just one more story about making changes, and I think you'll get the message.

"It was the early 1900s, and a young man named Clarence was taking his girlfriend on a summer outing. They took a picnic lunch out to a picturesque island in the middle of a small lake. She wore a long dress with about a dozen petticoats. He was dressed in a suit with a high collar.

"Clarence rowed them out to the island, dragged the boat onto shore, and spread their picnic supplies beneath a shade tree. So hypnotized was he by her beauty that he hardly noticed the hot sun and perspiration on his brow. Softly, she whispered to him, 'Clarence, you forgot the ice cream.'

"Never one to let down his favorite girl, Clarence pulled the boat back to the water and rowed to shore. He found a grocery store nearby, bought the ice cream and rowed back to the island. She batted her long eyelashes over her deep blue eyes and purred, 'Clarence, you forgot the chocolate syrup.'

"Now, love will make a person do strange things, but Clarence got back into that boat and returned to the store for syrup. And, as our hero Clarence rowed back toward the island, he suddenly stopped and sat there in the boat the rest of the afternoon, fascinated by an idea. By the end of that afternoon, Clarence Evinrude had invented the outboard motor. Oh, and by the way, Clarence later married the girl who waited so long on the island for the chocolate syrup – melted ice cream and all.

"Change may be difficult, but in this case, the changes Clarence Evinrude made have saved many of us from a heck of a lot of rowing."

ENDURE WHILE IMPROVING – SUMMARY

1. For every action, there is an equal and opposite reaction, so if your organization aims forward, expect backward motions from time to time.

2. It's productive to stop and evaluate what's working and what's not ... even when things are going well.

3. Change is painful and requires discipline and commitment – but in the long run, improvement cannot be made without change.

4. Eliminate stress-producing practices, which are activities that don't encourage productivity.

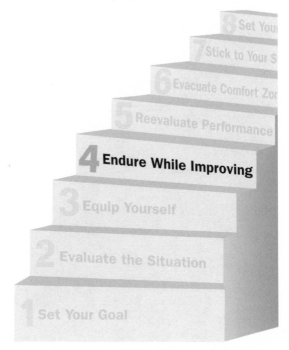

5 REEVALUATE PERFORMANCE:

A Proactive Mindset

"One who does not look ahead, remains behind."
– Brazilian Proverb

With their training at the midway point, Randy and Don were well on their way to achieving their goals. Their training regimens were balanced and each man was progressing steadily toward his goals, albeit not without the usual pains and strains.

On the sixth Saturday when the three met at the track, Michael was ready with a new challenge. "Before we run today, I want you to visualize every part of the run, from the warm-up to the point you feel you are at your best, and from that point to the end of the run and the cool down."

"I've heard about this visualization thing, but I've never tried it. It's a little 'out there' for me," Don confessed.

"Really, it's a pretty simple exercise. Just find a relaxed position. Some people like to sit, others lie down. Then, close your eyes, focus your thinking and picture what you look like … while you're warming up. Along with the physical picture, think about how it feels. When you're stretching during warm-up, how do your legs feel when you begin stretching and how do they feel when you're through stretching?

"How do you look when you're walking onto the track and up to the starting line? Think about all of your senses. How does it feel when you take a deep breath? How does the morning air smell?

"One thing about visualization," Michael pointed out, "it requires that you focus on things you may not have paid attention to before. For runners, I always like to ask how it feels when they pass someone … when they pass a prime competitor? How does it feel when you see the finish line in the distance? What happens to your body when you begin running that last 100 meters?

"Ready to try it?" Michael asked.

"Let's give it a go," Randy said, settling down into the grassy space next to the bleachers."

"I'm ready – but tell me the goal," said Don.

"Glad you asked that question," Michael responded, taking a seat next to the runners. "Visualization gives you a good idea of the 'soft' parts as well as the more difficult aspects of the run. As you visualize each part, you prepare yourself mentally for the experience."

"Sounds like a good tool – for anything," Don noted.

"Exactly. And, it won't surprise you that I've got a story to prove just how good a tool it is," Michael said.

The two younger men looked at each other knowingly and smiled. "You're right. We're not surprised … so let's hear it," Randy laughed.

"A few years back, during the off season, a basketball coach ran an experiment," Michael began. "He divided his team into two groups. He took one group into the gym and had them practice their free throws every day for one hour.

"While the first group was practicing shooting free throws, he took the second group into another gym, asked them to seat themselves in a comfortable position, close their eyes and visualize themselves shooting – and making – their free throws.

"The two groups spent time doing their assigned activities for a month and then the coach brought them back together to see how much they had improved. Surprisingly, the group that had been in the gym, practicing free throws, improved their shots by only 25 percent. The group that had visualized themselves making free throws, however, improved by more than 50 percent. Pretty interesting results, I'd say."

"That's pretty impressive," Don agreed.

"For runners, the power of visualization is an even better tool because not only can visualization help you run faster, it also serves as a tool for getting through the challenging parts of the race – like when it gets painful or during the last half mile," Michael explained. "In fact, I have a friend who, when she gets to a certain point and the pain is increasing, visualizes a battle going on in her head. On one side, is a little man called 'mind,' and another man called 'matter' is on the other side. She says they fight each other … until she crosses the finish line," Michael said. "It's her way of getting through the tough parts of the race."

"But, what if you're not so creative?" Randy wondered.

"Then you can make it through by visualizing yourself running smoothly, even if – in reality – it's getting more difficult to do so. By making visualization a part of your training, you prepare yourself for every part of the race and have the ability to recognize when the race is going to get tough, so you're ready to start your visualization."

"So, being proactive is part of reaching our goals?" asked Don.

"Right again … and let's talk about that after we finish your first visualization exercise and after our run today," Michael suggested as he stood and waited for his cohorts to join him on the track.

More than an hour later, the three had completed their training run, finished their cool down and were rehydrating on the bleachers.

"Ready to talk about the proactive mindset?" Michael wanted to know.

Don and Randy nodded.

"Okay. Here's the deal. Being proactive in running boils down to making things happen, not letting things happen to you," Michael explained. "If you know the last mile is going to be a killer, you need to have the tools to get through that last mile. Don't let it sneak up and surprise you.

"The same goes for business," he went on. "If you visualize what's ahead, you'll have the courage to keep going, to stay the course."

"I see what you mean," Don said. "Visualization becomes a good tool to be proactive in anything you do."

"Right you are ... and being proactive allows you to reevaluate in order to make things happen – instead of reacting to the things that happen to you.

"Several months ago, we had a company-wide employee survey," Michael continued. "Our management had all been describing the 'truth' as they thought we wanted it to be. However, the responses on the employee surveys didn't align with what we had been told. And, after tallying the results, I finally learned the real truth – what 'is' actually is."

"I remember the survey," Randy admitted, "and I also know some of my coworkers really said what they thought – about a lot of things. So, after the survey, what was your next move?"

"The survey results gave us the opportunity to deal with what is, not with what management wanted to know or what we thought we knew, but the truth about where our company really was," Michael responded. "When you discover the truth, it clears the way for you to reevaluate your situation so that you can move to the Next Level."

"I guess the next logical question is ... once you know the truth, how do you get to the Next Level?" Don questioned.

"Once you know what the truth is, you've got to have the courage to see reality – the truth – and then deal with it," Michael pointed out. "Once we got our arms around the truth about our company, we had to step back, talk to our people, make some adjustments, make some mistakes and recover quickly from them and then take some bold steps – some out-of-the-box maneuvers."

"Is that why your area began offering some of the new products that were just introduced this month?" Randy asked.

"That's the reason. We were soft in certain areas ... areas we realized were critical to our growth. So, we did some brainstorming, and interviews with our front-line employees and then came up with what we think will fill in those crucial gaps in our product line and our support services," Michael explained. "And, that brings me to the final step – being able to move your focus from 'the next big thing' to an emphasis on process improvements."

"Which is why you changed over your month-end processing a few weeks ago?" Don wanted to know.

"That's the reason," Michael replied. "We had been using the same process for more than four years, and we were missing out on some efficiencies that are now available to us. Sometimes improving a process requires a few tweaks here and there. Other times it means overhauling the entire system ... but the whole impetus comes from discovering the truth."

"So, if the truth about my running style is that I'm not as athletic as I should be to reach the goal I've set, then what do I need to do to reach the Next Level?" Randy asked as he put his running shoes into his gym bag.

"Well, I'm not ready to call that a truth," Michael said, "but if that were the case, moving to the Next Level might be as challenging as dropping a few pounds, increasing your stamina and then really overhauling your whole style of running. Or, it could be as simple as investing in a better pair of running shoes and carbing up before workouts and races."

The two men smiled. "The last approach really sounds more my speed," Randy admitted. ·

"Maybe so … but let me tell you about a group of proactive people – you may even be familiar with a couple of them. This story may surprise you," Michael promised.

"A few years ago, the National Football League and the NFL Players Association entered into agreements with Wharton and Harvard Business Schools to provide business education to NFL players," Michael related. "The whole purpose was to assist players in preparing for their post-playing careers.

"Okay, so imagine the nation's top quarterback coming to the end of his career. That's hard to accept, in itself. But, think about that quarterback – several years before his retirement – spending time in a classroom at Harvard or Wharton, learning what he needs to know about owning, operating or building his own business.

"Imagine transitioning from game days to 24-hour days of running your own business. Now, think about these players, really visualizing their futures and then trooping into classrooms to learn about entrepreneurship, investing, negotiation skills, risk management, real estate development and community reinvestment. It's a giant step for all of them, but they're being proactive in looking down the road, realizing they're not going to be at the top of their game forever. This opportunity assists them in focusing on being prepared when the time comes to make this daunting change from the spotlight and into the unknown territory of a totally different career."

"Awesome," said the two men in unison.

"I had no idea that was happening," Don admitted. "Pretty cool move on the part of the NFL."

"That's definitely something to think about – both personally and professionally, Randy said."

"One we all need to remember. Sometimes the truth and its possibilities are almost too difficult to even think about. What we want the truth to be is so much more palatable … but we need to look at every part of the picture, prepare ourselves for the challenges and keep tweaking the processes to get moving toward the Next Level," Michael said.

"As a simple exercise, why don't the two of you think about the various truths you find as you travel this road to the Next Level and let me know what you find. In the meantime, keep the vision," Michael said.

REEVALUATE PERFORMANCE – SUMMARY

1. Visualize the big picture and determine the real truths.

2. Embrace and address the truths … not what you want to believe, but what is … and reevaluate regularly.

3. Make adjustments and think outside the box to move ahead.

4. Once you've resumed your forward progress, think about your "next big thing."

6 EVACUATE COMFORT ZONES:

Choose to Grow

"Move out of your comfort zone. You can only grow if you are willing to feel awkward and uncomfortable when you try something new."
— Brian Tracy

As Michael suspected, by the seventh workout, his students were beginning to show signs of burnout – dragging themselves, dutifully, to the track – probably because he had offered to coach them. But, it was obvious, their hearts were somewhere else this particular Saturday, so he allowed them to take their time getting into the workout.

Randy was lacing his running shoes when he remembered the assignment from their last session. "You asked us to think about the truths we'd discovered as we were reaching for the Next Level, and I'll admit, I'm probably not too good in seeing truths all the time. I'd rather see things positively and only look for what I want to see. Some of the truths I've discovered aren't that positive."

"But, isn't that reality?" Don broke in.

Randy winced. "Well, yeah. But, if you see them, you really need to deal with them … and that's what I call 'dirty work.'"

"But, what's the alternative?" Michael asked.

"The alternative is like having a dead elephant in the middle of your living room and walking around it until it starts to smell. By that time, you really have an even bigger problem," Randy responded. "So, I've given this assignment a lot of thought, and this is what I came up with," he said, taking a folded piece of paper out of his gym bag.

"The truths about reaching the Next Level in my career include the following:

- ✦ I'm really not sure I would like everything that comes with a leadership role, especially when it comes time to have a difficult performance discussions with a member of the team.

- ✦ In my communications class, the ugly truth is that I don't always express my ideas very well.

- ✦ In my collaborations, I sometimes take on much more of the load than my collaborator … and then feel exploited later."

"You obviously did some soul searching on this one," Michael said, "and I appreciate you sharing these with us. As we said during the last time we met, truths are not always pretty, but once recognized, you need to embrace them and proactively adjust your performances and processes. So, how has that been going?"

Randy's usually smiling face was very serious now. "These truths, which are really hard for me to even admit, reflect areas in which I need to do a lot more work," he said. "If, for example, I'm not totally sure I would be a good leader, I need to be questioning whether the Next Level I've chosen is really the RIGHT Next Level for me. If I decide it's not – or if I get feedback that says I'm not really leadership material, then I need to change my focus."

"Not so fast," Michael interrupted. "You're letting yourself off the hook way too easily. What I hear you saying is that you see leadership as way out of your comfort zone … and frankly, I don't agree that you lack the qualities of a good leader. So, maybe if you embrace the truth that you may not like all that comes with the leadership role, take this truth and start working to resolve the hard parts. One of the best ways is to read books and attend seminars that give you more and better insights into the leadership role.

"If your truth points out soft spots, attack them with information, experiences and more experience," Michael concluded.

Randy nodded his understanding. "But, what about the other two truths – difficulty in expressing my ideas and taking on more than my collaborators and then feeling exploited?"

"I want you to tell me," Michael challenged.

"Well, I am taking a communications class at the college," Randy said. "Isn't that enough?"

"A college classroom is a fairly safe place," his mentor countered. "So, what about joining a Toastmasters Club where you have to make speeches regularly or lead the next corporate customer service meeting?

"To stop over extending yourself in collaborative efforts, I don't support giving 'til it hurts. Having said that, I think anyone – and particularly someone as conscientious as you – would want to make sure that goals set are eventually met. That may take more from you than your collaborators. In this 'truth,' your job is to recognize your abilities and your drive to make a meaningful contribution. At the end of the day, when your team wins, you win … and if you've given more than most, you can savor the victory that much more," Michael added.

"Makes sense," the younger man said. "I think my comfort zone is exactly that – comfortable – but I really do want to get to the Next Level. You make my truths sound definitely more embraceable."

Next it was Don's turn.

"I didn't bother to write these down, like Randy did," he apologized, "but I can definitely share some of the truths I've stumbled upon in my journey with my team to reach the Next Level … and I emphasize the term 'stumbled.'"

His compadres chuckled. Rarely did Don allow his "soft spots" to show long enough to be examined.

"When I took over the team, one of the members was struggling with a lot of problems at home. I gave him every leeway possible. However, he soon began having problems with coming to work – and after two or three additional conferences to find out what was going on and how I could help, I came to the point where I needed to fire him.

"The truth is, however, I allowed him to take advantage of my good nature way too long. As I tried to be understanding of his problems, some of the other members of the team were noticing how much he was getting away with. They began losing respect for my judgment … and, in fact, I'm sure I spent more time with that problem child than I did with some of my top producers."

"And, the truth about you as a leader is … ?" Michael wondered out loud.

"The truth is that my judgment, in this particular case, was way off and my team suffered," Don admitted.

"What you're really saying is that it was more comfortable to play the role of a good guy, no matter what the consequences were with the rest of the team, right?" Michael questioned.

Don's shoulders dropped like a guilty child's. "Nobody wants to be seen as an ogre, even by the person taking so much advantage of the goodness of your heart."

"Agreed," Randy piped up.

"But – and this is interesting – both of you have discovered truths about how far you'll go to avoid having to leave your individual comfort zones," Michael summarized, "and I'll leave it at that for awhile."

The two younger men looked at each other quizzically.

"All right," Michael said, changing the tone of their conversation. "I want to start this workout with one of my infamous stories." Seeing no protests, he began.

"Even though ours is a transient society, there are some people who live their entire lives in the same house they were born in. I've moved multiple times … so many, I can't tell you how many houses I've lived in without stopping to count up the many stops along my journey.

"In my humble estimation, rooms, houses and even cities all have their own energy fields, and while the energy of one place may serve us very well, at one point in our development it can be detrimental or totally uninspiring at another point in our lives.

"Depending on the time of our life, we need different fields of energy. Here's an example: When we started our family, we needed a home in a quiet little neighborhood in the city … a place where we felt secure and protected. Eventually, that home started feeling restrictive, as though it was closing in on us, so we moved to the country.

"Our country home, filled with the memories of our kids in their teenage years, is warm and inviting, but I imagine when our last child leaves, Pam and I will need the energy of another home in another setting.

"It is important that we are aware any time we receive signals that we may have energetically outgrown our current residence. Sometimes we stay in a living situation, not because it is inspiring but because it is convenient. And yet, to really grow … to really feel our best, we need to think beyond convenience. We need to commit to surrounding ourselves with the energetic qualities that must support our growth and well-being.

"Keeping that in mind, we're going to leave the comfort of the track today."

"So … where are we running?" asked Don.

"We're going to leave our comfort zones and widen our horizons," Michael said. "I'm taking you on the same route we ran during the corporate challenge."

For their workout that morning, Michael not only increased the distance of the run but he also increased the speed … something his students didn't realize until they had finished the workout and were cooling down as they walked back to the track.

"We were all so busy enjoying the new scenery, I forgot to mention I was increasing our distance today," Michael said, "so along with our run from the track to the start of the corporate challenge 5K course, we totaled more than four miles this morning.

"But, that's not all," Michael confessed. "I also pushed the pace so we were doing an easy seven-minute mile."

"Awesome," Randy murmured. "Didn't think I had it in me."

"Me either," Don admitted.

"As I mentioned in my story, sometimes it is beneficial to move from one 'house' to another so your energy can be resupplied or expanded, and it's also healthy to push yourself out of your comfort zone. Over the course of our Saturday workouts, the track became a comfort zone of sorts, and unfortunately, we don't always run in our comfort zone, from the standpoint of physical place or speed.

"In a typical 5K race, for example, you're probably going to run on a relatively unfamiliar course and you're also going to run at a faster pace. It's a natural response all of us experience when we get in a group of runners, all at different levels," Michael explained.

"I found that out during the last corporate challenge," Randy realized. "I was running at a much faster pace than I had ever trained at, and by the end of the race, I was sucking air, big time."

"That's pretty normal, especially if you haven't been training for a long period and your body hasn't been conditioned to 'feel' the pace that's comfortable for you," responded their mentor. "But, that comfort zone can also be lethal.

"A few years ago, a CEO of a major company told this story that really stuck with me: 'In bullfighting there is a term called *querencia*. The querencia is the spot in the ring to which the bull returns. Each bull has a different querencia, but as the bullfight continues, and the animal becomes more threatened, it returns more and more often to his spot. As he returns to his querencia, he becomes more predictable. And so, in the end, the matador is able to kill the bull because instead of trying something new, the bull returns to what is familiar. His comfort zone.'"

The two men nodded. "Good story," Don said. "I see what you mean by 'lethal' – and that, of course, could happen in your work life too … I suppose."

"Any time an organization's or an individual's strategy becomes predictable or the organization tires from running into roadblocks over and over again, they start retreating to the same position and, in doing so, become a target for their competitors – much like a bull in a bullring," Michael said. "This same truism applies to running a race, vying in a takeover attempt, applying for another position ... anything where competitors are part of the picture."

"Which is why it is important to think outside the box, to be innovative and to try new strategies," Randy added.

"Because it's not healthy to stay in your comfort zone," Don finished his partner's sentence.

"You've got it. Any organization that takes a predictable route is fair game. The same goes for the runner in a race. If you start off at the head of the pack and have no finish line strategy, you can bet there's someone just waiting and watching for you to start to lose speed or look tired. That's the predictability the CEO was talking about," Michael explained.

"Remember the corporate survey I spoke about?"

The two nodded.

"One of the respondents had this to say: 'Our biggest challenge to both maintain and grow the organization is to continually evolve in order to stay aligned with what the customer sees as value,'" Michael said.

"Wish I had said that," Randy added as he wiped the sweat from his face with his T-shirt.

"It was something that impressed all of us who looked at the results," Michael said, "and it reinforced our belief that we can't remain in a comfort zone too long before we move on to the next challenge. In a way, it justifies taking risks and trying new products and processes."

"But, how far out on the limb do you go before a risk becomes … well, too risky?" asked Don.

"Good question! Risk is something that's become part of the big picture for today's organizations that survive this rollercoaster economy. And, although it may not be obvious, it's part of running too, because the only way you can safely take risks is by having a trainer … a coach.

"Whenever we, as corporate leaders, take a few steps out on that proverbial limb, we're also talking to trainers, people who will – first of all – tell us the truth about where we are and where we need to go," Michael explained. "Working with a trainer takes out some of the risk from a new strategy, process or challenge of any type – although not all of it.

"These trainers are people who've run more races, know more strategies and can give us good advice and counsel," he continued. "They are people who may know nothing about our business but are experts in increasing revenues, motivating young talents and developing new customers."

The two nodded.

"There's also one more thing I've learned from my running coach, but I've learned it in my business career as well – and that's to stay in your own lane."

Don brightened. "That makes sense. You'll stay out of trouble if you stay in your own lane. You won't risk someone stepping on your heels or pushing you off the track, right?"

"Most of the time," Michael affirmed, "but there's another good reason to stay in your own lane, both literally and figuratively too.

"If you're running on a track and there are lane boundaries, you're also on the shortest course possible between the starting line and the finish line," he continued. "You can't be running all over the place. That's just adding distance for you that your competitors won't have to cover.

"Figuratively, staying in your own lane means focusing on the basics that are responsible for your success. A few years ago, one of the hot business trends was for corporations to expand their business reach by going into new areas. Sure, these new areas were related to their core business, but for the most part, they were also a new territory.

"What happened, as you may recall, was that some businesses stretched their resources way too far – like runners attempting to run a distance they hadn't prepared for before a race. Suddenly, they were breathing heavy – not literally, of course – but by expanding their reach, they found themselves separated from their core strengths and out of their 'hot spot' – separated from the abilities, savvy and know-how that had made them successful in the first place.

"Within five years of expanding product lines and service areas, many of these same corporations were moving back into their lanes to focus on their core businesses. Along with some of the businesses who reined in their scope, there were others that were so stretched out of shape, they could never acquire their initial successful forms and found, albeit too late, that they could not be all things to all people.

"The lesson: They thought by running in several other lanes or several lanes at one time, it would help them reach the Next Level. In reality, to reach the Next Level, you have to stay in your lane – the one that has been and will continue to be successful for you and your team."

"I guess that would go for us relative newcomers to the business arena," Don commented. "We should focus on our strengths, what has pushed us up through the ranks, right?"

"That old ambition of being all things to all people will only bring you down," Randy added.

"That's right … on both accounts … and in the actual race, staying in your own lane is the safest spot, the shortest distance around the track and the surest way of finishing the race ahead of the competition," Michael said, "but before you get involved in the rest of your Saturday, I have one more story I want to share that ties in with staying in your own lane."

"Here, I've got plenty of cold Gatorade in my cooler," Don offered. "I'm still feeling the effects of today's run."

"As long as you can drink and listen too," Michael joked. "My story is about eagles. During a vacation at the Grand Canyon several years ago, I found myself spending a lot of time with my binoculars, watching the eagles that were nesting in the canyon.

"I had never seen an eagle's nest before, but during that trip, I had an opportunity to see one, high in a crag of one of the cliffs. Unfortunately, I didn't get a glimpse inside, but one of the park rangers noticed my continued interest and told me a lot about eagles and their habits.

"When a mother eagle builds her nest, she starts with thorns, broken branches, sharp rocks and a number of other items that seem entirely unsuitable for the project. But, then she lines the nest with a thick padding of wool, feathers and fur from animals she has killed, making it soft and comfortable for the eggs.

"By the time her eaglets reach flying age, the comfort of the nest and the luxury of free meals make them quite reluctant to leave. That's when the mother eagle begins what the park ranger called 'stirring up the nest.' With her strong talons, she begins pulling out the thick carpet of fur and feathers, bringing the sharp rocks and thorns to the surface.

"As more of the bedding gets plucked up, the nest becomes more uncomfortable for the young eagles. Eventually, as the mother continues to stir the nest, along with other urgings, the eaglets are prompted to leave their once-comfortable abode and move on to more mature behavior, such as flight and hunting for food."

"So, it goes back to not hanging in your comfort zone too long," Randy observed. "That addresses the truths we reported before we started our run today."

"You guys are too quick ... but you get my point. And, the words for today are: 'Stay in your own lane but don't hang in your comfort zone too long,'" Michael said as he waved to his protégés. "... And, keep the vision," he added.

EVACUATE COMFORT ZONES – SUMMARY

1. Push yourself out of your comfort zone and into greater challenges. When an organization's strategy becomes predictable, they are a sitting target for their competitors.

2. To maintain and grow, the organization is to stay aligned with what customers and/or stakeholders see as value.

3. Risk is part of the big picture. To safely take risks is having people who know nothing about our business but are experts in increasing revenue, motivating young talent and developing new customers on our team.

4. Staying in your own lane means focusing on the basics responsible for your success, but don't hang in your comfort zone too long.

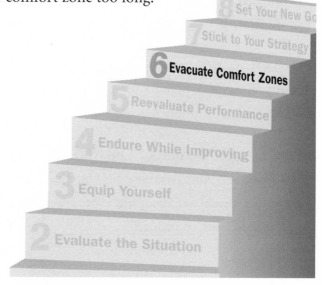

7
STICK TO YOUR STRATEGY:

Ne Sim Obex

"You are capable of more than you know. Choose a goal that seems right for you and strive to be the best, however hard the path. Prepare to be alone at times, and to endure failure, but persist! The world needs all you can give."
– Edward O. Wilson, Harvard Scientist and Pulitzer Prize Winner

The last Saturday the threesome had planned to work out together, all three men arrived at the track early. Over the months spanned by their workouts, they had developed a bond of appreciation for what each brought to the group.

Michael, as the mentor, was seen as a sort of ultimate leader, with a wealth of experience and the unique ability to push his students beyond what they ever thought they could accomplish. Don, a willing student, was the more analytical, wanting to understand the concept before actually employing it. And Randy ... well, Randy was the hard worker. Always smiling, Randy had little in the way of natural athletic ability and had put in much more than his counterpart in his effort to make his goals his reality.

As a group, they fit together as three unique pieces in a jigsaw puzzle – and over the past months, they had come to appreciate their individual uniqueness, drawing from each other to make every workout a stepping stone to their own Next Level.

As they sat in the grass next to the bleachers, putting on their running shoes, Michael pulled something out of his gym bag that caught the glint of the early morning sun. "Since this is our last day, I wanted you guys to see this," he began, passing the round object to Don.

"Someone gave it to me years ago and challenged me to make it part of my leadership mantra," he explained.

Don looked at the round disk carefully. One side was blank. On the other was the Latin phrase, "*Ne Sim Obex.*"

"It's been a long time since my Latin classes in high school," Don admitted, "and I'm not familiar with these words." He passed the disk to Randy.

"When the gentleman gave me the disk, he shared some advice that had been handed down by one of his own mentors," Michael explained. "Ne Sim Obex – May I not be an obstacle."

The two students were quiet for a moment. "An effective leader is someone who doesn't impede his or her followers … is that the meaning?" Don wanted to know.

"Exactly. In organizations as well as other parts of life, sometimes leaders become their own worst enemies because they prevent their people from performing," Michael explained. "Working with both of you over the last several months, I sense that you put as much into your goals at work as you do in your goals for improving your running styles … and because you have been so focused on reaching the Next Level in the next 5K corporate challenge, one of the things I've been working to avoid is becoming an obstacle.

"As a coach and mentor, I don't want to move you along too quickly, but I also don't want to move so slowly that you burn out. I want to provide challenges when you're ready to reach the Next Level in your running, but I don't want to overwhelm you with impossible tasks, either," he continued. "My challenge is to maintain your momentum and your steady achievement without becoming an obstacle in the process."

"Now that we're discussing this, I have had a manager in my career that – in spite of what I considered to be his good intentions – was an obstacle. His personal issues at home eventually translated into issues with upper management," Don recalled. "In short order, most of us had put in for transfers to other teams because we began seeing him as a stumbling block, an obstacle."

"I'd like to hear more about that experience," Michael said.

"Essentially, whenever one of us wanted to move ahead, he held us back. He discouraged innovation and took the bows when any of the team members came up with a unique idea."

Randy nodded. "I've seen that before … not often, but you know it when you see it. It's not that the manager is trying to be an obstacle, he just wants to be the one with all the good ideas. That prevents people who come up with a better way from getting the credit they deserve. That is not Ne Sim Obex, but it's frustrating and it's a good way to scare off the best talents on your team … which is what happened."

"On the other hand, there's something to be said about overcoming obstacles – even if that obstacle is your boss or your coach," Michael pointed out. "In 1962, Victor and Mildred Goertzel published a revealing study of 413 'famous and exceptionally gifted people' called *Cradles of Eminence*. They spent years attempting to understand what produced greatness, what common thread might run through the lives of all these outstanding people. Surprisingly, the most outstanding fact was that virtually all of them, about 392, had to overcome very difficult obstacles in order to become who they were. So, within this context, obstacles are totally positive experiences … for certain individuals.

"Well, before we get out on the track this morning, I want to talk racing strategy with you." Michael explained. "When I first started running in 5Ks and 10Ks, I never had a strategy, but after I started working with a coach, I learned that not having a strategy is like trying to run a race in a pair of running shoes that don't fit. You'll get blisters … and you'll never win."

"But, do you really have to have a strategy to start running when the gun sounds and then running long enough to cross the finish line?" Randy wondered aloud.

"Oh sure, you can do it without a strategy, but you'll also have to be satisfied with finishing at the back of the pack," Michael said.

"So, what's the strategy?" Don asked.

"Really, it's pretty simple. It's all about running your own race. It's about starting at a speed that's familiar … and, really, it's about the speed you've rehearsed each time you run. It's about knowing what your body is able to do and how long your body is able to do it.

"The other day, I watched the 3200 meter event during the Penn Relays," Michael continued. "The runners know how many laps they will run, what speed they need to run and how much they should have left to sprint the last 200 meters or more. Some of the runners start at the front of the pack. Others prefer to hang toward the back of the pack and then make their move to the front during the last 400 meters. Whatever strategy they use, their goal is to be the first over the finish line. It's knowing what their bodies can do, what works best for them and then, of course, considering the competition.

"If you know a runner is going to begin their sprint during the next to the last lap, you figure that into your strategy. If you know you're only going to have enough 'juice' left to sprint the last lap, you leverage your energy with a good strategy. The moral of this story – you've got to have a plan before you line up at the starting line," Michael concluded.

His two students nodded. "So, what's your strategy?" Don asked.

"The week before any race, you should be doing what we call 'tapering.' The week before the race, you should pull back to one or two easy, short runs and then give your body plenty of time to recover. That's the first part of the strategy.

"A few days before the race, you should begin hydrating more … making a concerted effort to drink more water than usual. Then, the day before the race, make certain you have some good carb intake. A bunch of us usually meet at one of the local Italian restaurants and have spaghetti the night before the race. But, we meet early so we can go home and get a good night's sleep. All of this is part of the strategy.

"I know some runners who work out hard the week before the race. Then, when time for the race comes, their legs are heavy and they run out of steam before they reach the finish line," Michael said. "The problem was that they didn't have a good strategy … and a good strategy is key to being successful. But before I tell you a good story, let's stretch and get on the track."

That morning as the three began their first lap, Michael was amazed in the improvement of his two students. Both were striding well, their forms were good and their pace was more than manageable. He would be sure to share his observations with them after the run.

"So, what about your story?" Don asked.

"Okay, here it is. Several years ago, a friend of mine told me a story about trying to get a job in a logging camp over the summer while he was a college student. When he asked the foreman for a job, the guy – a gruff veteran replied, 'Let's see you fell this tree first.'

"My friend, who came from a long line of loggers, stepped forward and skillfully felled a great tree. Impressed, the foreman exclaimed, 'Start Monday!'

"Monday, Tuesday, Wednesday, Thursday rolled by, and Thursday afternoon the foreman approached my friend and said, 'You can pick up your paycheck on the way out today.'

"Startled, this eager college student replied, 'I thought you paid on Friday.'

"'Normally we do,' answered the foreman, 'but we're letting you go today because you've fallen behind. Our daily felling charts show that you've dropped from first place on Monday to last on Wednesday.'

"'But I'm a hard worker,' my friend argued. 'I arrive first, leave last, and have even worked through my coffee breaks!'

"The foreman thought for a minute and then asked, 'Have you been sharpening your ax?' The young man replied, 'I've been working too hard to take the time.'"

"Your friend didn't have much of a strategy," Randy observed.

"Not one that included taking time to sharpen his axe," Michael agreed. "And that story has stayed with me, not only in my running career but in my business life, as well. You have to keep your axe sharpened, you never know when your next big opportunity will come up. You don't want to be out of energy before you reach the finish line."

"Okay, I'm beginning to see how a strategy is important," Don said, "so once we're in the race, should we work to get to the head of the pack or is there a better way?"

"Well, first of all, remember that a winner paces himself. A loser has only two speeds – hysterical and lethargic," Michael pointed out. "If using the best pace – the one you've run in practice – you can move to the head of the pack, there are some advantages to doing that, but I'll go back to what I said earlier and that is the best strategy is to run your own race.

"You may be one of those people who need to hear footsteps behind you in order to run your best race. Sometimes competition breathing down your neck is a strong motivation. On the other hand, you may also be one of those people who automatically feel defeated as soon as people start passing and getting several strides ahead of you.

"In planning your strategy, be really honest with yourself," Michael emphasized.

"In what areas?" Randy wanted to know.

"First of all, you need to decide where you are in your running. Since both of you have run relatively few 5Ks, it's fair to say you're relative novices – and you need to take that into your planning," Michael pointed out.

"Second, how have your practices gone before the race? Are you feeling pretty good about where you are? Are you seeing a spike in your stamina?

"Third, where are you in your visualizations? Do you see yourself at the front of the pack ... or do you see yourself finishing well behind the front runners? All of these play into the strategy you develop for each race – and, of course, every race will require a different strategy because we'll assume that, with every race, you'll move to the Next Level in terms of experience, racing savvy, how your body reacts to race-day jitters and other facets of racing that will come up ... like, are you able to run with people you know, people you trust. I could go on and on."

"This all makes sense," Randy said, "which gives me some good clues about why I haven't done well in past races. I just didn't have the information I needed nor the practice it takes to move up."

"It's the same when it comes to your career," Michael explained.

"To reach the Next Level, you need to have a strategy, you need to visualize what you want, you need to put in time training and you need to run your own race."

"That makes sense to me too," Don replied, "and you need a leader that doesn't become an obstacle."

Michael smiled. "Absolutely. You guys are getting ahead of me, but I want to share just a few more pointers with you as we cool down:

1. **If you aspire to a leadership position, make sure you 'train' for the job.** And by that I mean, make sure your work history contains enough of the responsibilities that provide the experience you really need. If you don't have some of the experiences required for the Next Level, find out how to get them. Just like in your running, once you've had the experience of three or four 5Ks, you're not only going to cross the finish line sooner, but you'll also have a keener picture of what you need to do to get even better for the next race.

2. **Take charge of your own development.** As you've seen, working with a coach is a good way to speed your development along as a runner. Most of us need a coach, at least to get us started down the right path. It's similar in business," Michael continued. "You have to be proactive and take the initiative in your own professional development. Some people hire career coaches. Others find what they need to know in books.

Being proactive means asking your boss questions during your performance review like, 'What do I have to do to get ahead? What are my shortcomings, and how can I address them? How can I build further on my strengths?' Your boss should suggest specific kinds of training or particular stretch assignments that will help you fill gaps in your skills and make you more promotable.

3. **Move beyond status quo.** Some people who run 5Ks aspire to run marathons," Michael pointed out. "Never lose sight of your current position and your current goals because you may miss out on some of the basics you need to build to the Next Level. In my own experience, I've seen too many aspiring leaders spend way too much time and energy campaigning for their next job when they should be knocking the ball out of the park with their current job.

4. **Read and learn something new every day.** In order to get to the top of your running game, find out what other people are saying and doing. Read about other people's training regimens. Find out more about nutrition. Learn the pros and cons about the various types of running shoes – and try to develop a network of fellow runners, people you can train with, who will tell you about other races, those you won't want to miss and those you want to avoid. To find opportunities in business, you not only need to read voraciously, but you will also want to have a network that you create from people you meet at industry forums, conventions, trade shows or college classes.

5. **Be your own mentor.** Everyone could use an older, wiser adviser at least some of the time on his or her career journey. We all need someone to show us the ropes, someone to explain, behind closed doors, what's really happening,"

Michael said, "but we also need to learn how to help ourselves develop along the way. Working with a mentor or coach is always beneficial, but sometimes we have to depend on ourselves and our gut instincts to get where we want to go. Learn how to find out what is required, how am I doing, does anyone care, how is the team doing and where do we fit in?

"Reaching the Next Level, however you define it, doesn't just happen. It takes vision, discipline and action, as you've learned during our training sessions," Michael concluded as the trio returned to the bleachers.

"Man, I've got to get home so I can write these down," Randy said. "You've just answered questions I've had for a long time."

"Me too," said Don. "Questions about running as well as about where my career's going next."

Michael chuckled. "The great part is that you can apply much of what you've learned to almost any situation where you're working to reach the Next Level. It all applies. But, in the meantime, let's get together for a couple of long runs before the corporate challenge," he suggested. "That'll give you time to fine tune what you're doing."

The three men shook hands and walked toward the parking lot.

"Oh, Michael," Randy called. "Remember to keep the vision."

STICK TO YOUR STRATEGY – SUMMARY

1. Don't be an obstacle to anyone or any effort to reach the Next Level. An effective leader doesn't impede his or her followers.

2. Don't move your team along too quickly, but also don't move so slowly that the team burns out. Provide challenges when the team is ready to reach the Next Level, but don't overwhelm them with impossible tasks.

3. You can't wait for opportunities. You have to have a strategy, so when opportunities arise, you'll have a sharp axe and enough energy to reach the finish line.

4. Reaching the Next Level doesn't just happen. It takes vision, discipline and action.

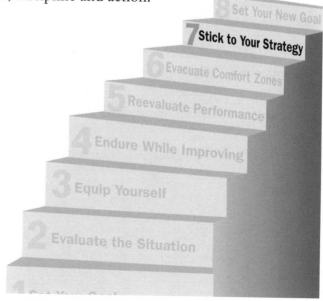

8 SET YOUR NEW GOAL:

On to the Next Level

*"The higher you have to reach, the deeper you have to dig —
moving to the Next Level comes from this process."*
— Unknown

At the next 5K corporate challenge, a large crowd gathered at the finish line to welcome the runners and, once again, Michael Burney was the first to cross the finish line, achieving another personal best time as he broke the tape.

Of the three, Don was the next in, running his race at a comfortable pace. Randy was right behind him. Both students finished in the top 25, shaving more than a minute and a half off their previous race pace. They were obviously pleased with their performances as they joined their coach for a banana and Gatorade in the refreshment tent.

"Man, I couldn't believe the difference," Randy beamed. "Last year I was in terrible shape after the race. Today, I feel like I could run another 5K – after a short rest anyway."

"I'm getting closer to where I want to be," Don said, "but this was, as you said Michael, a great experience. I'll continue to build on this as I work out for the next race."

"It's been a good experience for me too," Michael admitted. "There's an old saying that goes something like, when you teach, you learn – and believe me, I have. Thanks, guys."

"So, what about a story," Randy said. "We can't let a chance for a story go by. We're conditioned now."

"Well, we all know how it feels to run a 5K. Next, we should start training together for a 10K and then after that, we'll train for this special race the Greeks had in their Olympic games that was unique. The winner was not the runner who finished first. It was the runner who finished with his torch still lit. Any takers?" Michael smiled.

His two students looked around. "Nope, not here. Not now, at least."

"So, what have you learned out of all these meetings that will most impact your life – not just your running life but your business and private life, as well? Michael asked.

There was silence … a long silence before Don spoke. "I think the biggest lesson I've learned and want to share with my team is to avoid hanging around your comfort zone too long. Without taking risks, you'll never get to the Next Level."

Randy nodded. "I'm going to remember that one, but I think I'm also going to try being more proactive about my development – not just in running but also in what I bring to the table in my career. I've been too content, waiting for things to happen, waiting for opportunities to be served at my desk. If I'm going to reach the Next Level, I'll need to change my approach – which hasn't gotten me as far as I thought I could go."

"I'm glad you both are enjoying walking along this ledge," Michael said, "because you get a better view of what's happening. I also knew a housewife who decided to walk along the same scary ledge. Her name was Bette Nesmith.

"Back in the 1960s, Bette was a single mom and a secretary in a Dallas bank when she decided there could be a better way to correct typing errors than using a clumsy typing eraser. And, in those days, typists used carbon paper because not everyone had copiers onsite, so when errors were made, the typist had to correct all the copies.

"Putting her art experience to work, Bette knew artists just painted over their errors. After several trials, using her kitchen blender, she concocted a fluid that matched the bank's letterhead to make it possible to paint over typing errors.

"Before long, all the secretaries in her building were using what she then called 'MistakeOut.' They were so crazy about her product, they urged Bette to sell her idea to various companies (including IBM), but they all turned her down. However, secretaries at the bank and from other businesses continued to ask for her product, so she converted her kitchen into her first manufacturing facility and started selling MistakeOut on her own. Later, thanks to her persistence and perseverance, she moved her company to the Next Level and into a 35,000-sq. ft. building with equipment designed to produce 500 bottles of her product every minute.

"When Bette Nesmith sold the enterprise in 1979, the tiny white bottles of what she now called 'Liquid Paper' were earning $3.5 million annually on sales of $38 million. The buyer was Gillette Corporation and the sale price was $47.5 million.

"With some of her earnings, Bette established a foundation to help single working mothers attend college and obtain the tools they needed to reach the Next Level. That foundation lived after Bette, who – unfortunately – died six months after she sold her company."

"Awesome story," Randy smiled. "In fact, I think I may have seen some Liquid Paper on my mom's desk when she was a secretary."

"Michael, you never let us down – you have stories for everything," Don commented. "Maybe you should write some of this stuff down."

"Maybe I should – like my friend should have stopped long enough to sharpen his axe, but I'll think about it. Maybe when I get too old to run, I'll put some of these stories on paper ... but in the interim, I would rather spend my free time coaching people to the Next Level. You guys have really gotten me fired up."

"Oh, really," said Don. "Fired up enough to help me get ready for next year's marathon?"

Michael paused for a moment. "A marathon, eh? Are you sure?"

"Sure as I'm standing here. That's my next goal ... and remember, you were the one that said we continue reaching for the Next Level as part of our human nature," Don affirmed.

"Mine too," Randy said and then added, "I can't believe it, but I think running a marathon would be too cool!"

"Okay guys – you've only taken baby steps in running until now, and I'll warn you, it's going to be rough, much harder than training for a 5K," Michael warned.

"We're ready," the two said in unison.

"To be honest, I've been thinking about trying a marathon next year, myself," their mentor admitted. "So, I guess we'd better get started."

"How about next Saturday?" Don suggested.

"Sounds good to me," Michael said.

"Me too," Randy echoed. "On to the Next Level."

8 Set Your New Goal
7 Stick to Your Strategy
6 Evacuate Comfort Zones
5 Reevaluate Performance
4 Endure While Improving
3 Equip Yourself
2 Evaluate the Situation
1 Set Your Goal

SUMMARY

Requirements to Reach the Next Level

1. Desire to improve

2. Understand there is room for improvement

3. Confidence that positive change can happen

Stepping Up to the Challenge

1. The Next Level – in anything – is more than one element of performance. It's the big picture.

2. To move to the Next Level you must:
   + Set your goal
   + Evaluate the situation
   + Equip yourself
   + Endure while improving
   + Reevaluate performance
   + Evacuate comfort zones
   + Stick to your strategy
   + Set your new goal

3. Taking a step back is sometimes necessary before moving up to the Next Level.

4. Getting to the Next Level doesn't just happen. It takes vision, discipline and action, but taking steps toward systemic change can be the most powerful aspect of this process.

Set Your Goal: Stretch Objectives

1. Getting to the Next Level is about balance – sharpening obvious skills, honing secondary skills and maintaining balance between people skills and professional skills.

2. Taking steps toward the Next Level can be the most painful and also the most powerful aspect of any change.

3. If you want a place in the sun, expect some blisters.

4. Moving to the Next Level includes the possibility of having to give up something … and that "something" differs with every goal.

Evaluate the Situation: Who, What, When

1. Identify opponents preventing you from reaching the Next Level … and then develop remedies.

2. Identify goals and strategize focus. Those team members satisfied with status quo should be (a) brought up to speed or (b) encouraged to transfer.

3. Teach the business of the business by exploiting operational business intelligence and achieving teams of the right people with the right information.

4. Multiply the power of one by the number of strong members on your team.

Equip Yourself: Duck and (Re)Cover

1. Equipping for the Next Level means being able to recover from unexpected adversity.

2. Create a contingency plan on how you will react to an unexpected crisis.

3. Understanding the "business of your business" creates ownership for your team members.

4. Collaborations are important for accomplishing goals and celebrating the achievement.

Endure While Improving: Courage to Change

1. For every action, there is an equal and opposite reaction, so if your organization aims forward, expect backward motions from time to time.

2. It's productive to stop and evaluate what's working and what's not … even when things are going well.

3. Change is painful and requires discipline and commitment – but in the long run, improvement cannot be made without change.

4. Eliminate stress-producing practices, which are activities that don't encourage productivity.

Reevaluate Performance: A Proactive Mindset

1. Visualize the big picture and determine the real truths.

2. Embrace and address the truths … not what you want to believe, but what is … and reevaluate regularly.

3. Make adjustments and think outside the box to move ahead.

4. Once you've resumed your forward progress, think about your "next big thing."

Evacuate Comfort Zones: Courage to Grow

1. Push yourself out of your comfort zone and into greater challenges. When an organization's strategy becomes predictable, they are a sitting target for their competitors.

2. To maintain and grow, the organization is to stay aligned with what customers and/or stakeholders see as value.

3. Risk is part of the big picture. To safely take risks is having people who know nothing about our business but are experts in increasing revenue, motivating young talent and developing new customers on our team.

4. Staying in your own lane means focusing on the basics responsible for your success, but don't hang in your comfort zone too long.

Stick to Your Strategy: Ne Sim Obex

1. Don't be an obstacle to anyone or any effort to reach the Next Level. An effective leader doesn't impede his or her followers.

2. Don't move your team along too quickly, but also don't move so slowly that the team burns out. Provide challenges when the team is ready to reach the Next Level, but don't overwhelm them with impossible tasks.

3. You can't wait for opportunities. You have to have a strategy so when opportunities arise, you'll have a sharp axe and enough energy to reach the finish line.

4. Reaching the Next Level doesn't just happen. It takes vision, discipline and action.

Set Your New Goal!

Five ways to bring
The Next Level
message to your team:

1. *The Next Level* **PowerPoint® Presentation**
   Introduce and reinforce *The Next Level* to your organization with this complete and cost-effective companion presentation piece. All the main concepts and ideas in the book are reinforced in this professionally produced, downloadable **PowerPoint presentation with facilitator guide and notes.** Use the presentation for kick-off meetings, training sessions or as a follow-up development tool. **$99.95**
   Participant Guides Pk/20 **$49.95**

2. **Keynote Presentation**
   Invite author and speaker David Cottrell to help your team reach *The Next Level.* David has inspired people to peak performance for more than 25 years. He delivers fast moving, practical ideas that can be implemented immediately to get results. For more information, visit www.DavidCottrell.com.

3. *The Next Level* **Learning Reinforcement Kit**
   Includes one each of *The Next Level* book, reminder card and quick reference desktop tent. **$19.95**

4. *The Next Level* **Quick Reference Desktop Tent**
   3½" x 6" Pk/20 **$59.95**

5. *The Next Level* **Reminder Card**
   5" x 7", laminated. Pk/20 **$19.95**

Accelerate Team Performance Package

I Quit, But Forgot to Tell You provides the straightforward, logical truths that lead to disengagement ... and provides the antidotes to prevent the virus from spreading within your organization. **$14.95**

Power Exchange – How to Boost Accountability & Performance in Today's Workforce This quick read offers practical strategies to help any leader boost accountability and performance in today's workforce. **$9.95**

Passionate Performance ... Engaging Minds and Hearts to Conquer the Competition offers practical strategies to engage the minds and heart of your team at home, work, church or community. Read it and conquer your competition! **$9.95**

Monday Morning Communications provides workable strategies to solving serious communications challenges. **$14.95**

180 Ways to Walk the Recognition Talk will help you provide recognition to your people more often and more effectively. **$9.95**

Lessons in Loyalty takes you inside Southwest Airlines to discover what makes it so different ... and successful. **$14.95**

The Manager's Coaching Handbook is a practical guide to improve performance from your superstars, middle stars and falling stars. **$9.95**

Start Right – Stay Right is every employee's straight talk guide to personal responsibility and job success. Perfect for every employee at every level. **$9.95**

Ouch! That Stereotype Hurts Regardless of your job title, you need to communicate with others to be successful. If you want to communicate respect through your message so that you can help build a workplace where all individuals feel included, this book is for you! **$12.95**

The Manager's Communication Handbook will allow you to connect with employees and create the understanding, support and acceptance critical to your success. **$9.95**

The NEW CornerStone Perpetual Calendar, a compelling collection of quotes about leadership and life, is perfect for office desks, school and home countertops. **$14.95**

CornerStone Collection of Note Cards Sampler Pack is designed to make it easy for you to show appreciation for your team, clients and friends. The awesome photography and your personal message written inside will create a lasting impact. Pack of 12 (one each of all 12 designs) **$24.95**

Visit www.CornerStoneLeadership.com for additional books and resources.

Recommended Resources for Additional Study:

Requirements to Reach the Next Level
  12 Choices … That Lead to Your Success by David Cottrell **$14.95**

Stepping Up to the Challenge
  *Passionate Performance: Engaging Minds and Hearts
  to Conquer the Competition* by Lee J. Colan **$9.95**

Set Your Goal: Stretch Objective
  Goal Setting for Results by Gary Ryan Blair **$9.95**

Evaluate the Situation: Who, What, When
  Management Insights by Ken Carnes, David Cottrell
  and Mark Layton **$14.95**

Equip Yourself: Duck and (Re)Cover
  Conquering Adversity by Christopher Novak **$14.95**

Endure While Improving: Courage to Change
  Leadership Courage by David Cottrell and Eric Harvey **$14.95**

Reevaluate Performance: A Proactive Mindset
  Monday Morning Leadership by David Cottrell **$14.95**

Evacuate Comfort Zones: Choose to Grow
  The Ant and the Elephant by Vince Poscente **$12.95**

Stick to Your Strategy: Ne Sim Obex
  Sticking to It: The Art of Adherence by Lee J. Colan **$9.95**

Set Your New Goal: On to the Next Level
  *Power Exchange: How to Boost Accountability
  & Performance in Today's Workforce* by Lee J. Colan **$9.95**

Visit www.**CornerStoneLeadership**.com
for additional books and resources

Order Form

1-30 copies $14.95	31-100 copies $13.95	100+ copies $12.95

The Next Level _____ copies X _____ = $_____

The Next Level Companion Resources

PowerPoint® Presentation (downloadable) _____ copies X $99.95 = $_____

Participant Guides (Pk/20) _____ pack(s) X $49.95 = $_____

Quick Reference Desktop Tent (Pk/20) _____ pack(s) X $59.95 = $_____

Reminder Cards (pk/20) _____ pack(s) X $19.95 = $_____

The Next Level Learning Reinforcement Kit _____ kit(s) X $19.95 = $_____
(Includes one each of *The Next Level,* Reminder
Card, and Quick Reference Desktop Tent)

Accelerate Team Performance Resources

Accelerate Team Performance Package _____ pack(s) X $149.95 = $_____
(Includes one copy of *The Next Level* and one
each of the items listed on page 125)

Other Books

_____ _____ copies X _____ = $_____

_____ _____ copies X _____ = $_____

_____ _____ copies X _____ = $_____

Shipping & Handling $_____

Subtotal $_____

Sales Tax (8.25%-TX Only) $_____

Total (U.S. Dollars Only) $_____

Shipping and Handling Charges

Total $ Amount	Up to $50	$51-$99	$100-$249	$250-$1199	$1200-$2999	$3000+
Charge	$6	$9	$16	$30	$80	$125

Name _____ Job Title _____

Organization _____ Phone _____

Shipping Address _____ Fax _____

Billing Address _____ Email _____
(required when ordering PowerPoint® Presentation)

City _____ State_____ ZIP _____

❑ Please invoice (Orders over $200) Purchase Order Number (if applicable) _____

Charge Your Order: ❑ MasterCard ❑ Visa ❑ American Express

Credit Card Number _____ Exp. Date _____

Signature _____

❑ Check Enclosed (Payable to: CornerStone Leadership)

Mail

Phone 888.789.5323
Fax 972.274.2884   www.**CornerStoneLeadership**.com

P.O. Box 764087
Dallas, TX 75376

Thank you for reading *The Next Level*.
We hope it has assisted you in your quest for
personal and professional growth.

CornerStone Leadership is committed to provide new
and enlightening products to organizations worldwide.
Our mission is to fuel knowledge with practical resources
that will accelerate your team's productivity,
success and job satisfaction!

Best wishes for your continued success.

CornerStone
Leadership Institute
www.CornerStoneLeadership.com

*Start a crusade in your organization –
have the courage to learn, the vision to lead,
and the passion to share.*